People in Period

GEORGIAN PEOPLE

FRED DWYER

B T Batsford Ltd *London*

General Editor
Dr James L. Henderson
formerly at Institute of Education
University of London
and Chairman, The World Education
Fellowship.

First published 1978
© Fred Dwyer 1978

ISBN 0 7134 0045 5

Printed and bound in Great Britain by
Cox & Wyman, Fakenham
for the Publishers B T Batsford Ltd
4 Fitzhardinge Street, London W1H 0AH

ACKNOWLEDGMENT

The Author and Publishers thank the
following for their kind permission to
reproduce copyright illustrations: David &
Charles Ltd for figs 33-5; Mary Evans Picture
Library for figs 42 and 44; the Hunterian
Museum (Royal College of Surgeons of
England) for figs 11, 14, 16 and 17; the
Mansell Collection for figs 10, 22, 23, 25
and 27; the National Portrait Gallery for
figs 2, 3 and 4; the Pharmaceutical Society
Museum for fig 7; Radio Times Hulton
Picture Library for figs 9, 12, 13, 15, 18-21,
24, 26, 29, 31, 32, 37-41, 43 and 45-7;
Ann Ronan Picture Library for figs 5, 6,
and 8; and Wigan Leisure Department for
fig 36. The other pictures appearing in this
book are the property of the Publishers.

Contents

List of illustrations

INTRODUCTION

History is about people. Stories of ordinary people, told in their own words in a lively way, can recapture the atmosphere of times past more effectively than accounts of famous individuals whose extraordinary achievements make them seem larger than life. The men and women who feature in this book left diaries and journals which we can easily consult. I chose these particular people because they represent types within the society of Georgian England, whose local day to day experiences reflect aspects of the larger national scene.

It is no accident that four of them lived in the north-west of England. In this period Lancashire and the West Riding began to emerge as an industrial region which was quite different from the agricultural and rural world elsewhere. Liverpool was beginning to grow in Blundell's day. By the time we get to Stubs and Ellen Weeton it is rivalling London and Bristol as a port, with a powerful interest in shipbuilding and the slave trade. Nearby Manchester has trebled in population since 1760 and places further afield like Sheffield and Birmingham have become industrial centres in their own right. When Miss Weeton travelled to Liverpool by canal boat and crossed the Mersey on a paddle steamer she saw the transport and industrial revolutions all round her!

Squire Blundell and Doctor Kay lived in the first half of the eighteenth century when the pace of life was slower, but even they saw many changes — some would say revolutions — in farming and in medicine. They saw something of rebellion too in the Jacobite risings, but this involvement in national politics was exceptional. Normally the life of ordinary citizens was not disturbed by central government; they lived instinctively according to the old ways, content with institutions which had ruled them for generations. Blundell, Kay and Stubs knew all their dependants — whether tenants, patients or workmen — as if they were part of one large family, and accepted responsibility for them.

In this apparently genial world the gentry and upper classes cultivated their estates and enlarged their country houses. They visited the pleasant inland spas, enjoyed the London season and at some time in their lives made the Grand Tour of the Continent. This was the world of Lady Betty Berkeley, one of elegance and indolence. But when we look into the lives of the mass of the people we realize that nothing could be further from the truth. Georgian England could also be a hard place, cruel and vulgar, where human life was cheap. Captain Carter and Private Wheeler knew that death might strike at any time. The crowds which watched executions at Tyburn and whippings at the Bridewell might themselves be victims of riot or disease. Bloodthirsty sporting contests were a national passion. It was a country undergoing a revolution in more ways than one.

The religious revolution of Methodism at first met the hostility of the ruling class, disturbed by the enthusiasm roused by preachers like Adam Clarke. Later they saw that the emphasis on discipline and hard work was a help towards public order. Twenty years of warfare in the middle of the century bred a restless and confident outlook. Merchants were calling for a 'Blue Water Policy' bringing commercial profit and imperial expansion. Population was growing and food production increasing; all branches of trade and industry seemed to be flourishing. The mood was one of aggressive patriotism, with France the national enemy. Both Carter and Wheeler thought themselves worth ten Frenchmen. So confident were we that we lost one empire to the Americans and won another from France and Spain within a generation.

Within this exciting picture the graceful form of Betty Berkeley moves with an ambitious irrelevance, searching for a place in the circle surrounding the Prince of Wales; he himself is fretting at his exclusion by a father occasionally incapacitated by a malady once described by his mystified doctor as 'the flying gout'. As the country struggled through its greatest war, with

1   George I (born 1660, reigned 1714-1727).   2   George II (born 1683, reigned 1727-1760).

millions suffering the new evils of industrialism, those members of the Regency aristocracy who were not with Wellington found that their blind extravagance had earned them the hatred of the nation.

It is unlikely that the characters in this book ever met another of their company. Religion would have deterred Blundell and Kay from mutual interests, although it might have brought Clarke and Carter together in the Channel Isles in 1786. Betty Berkeley and Sergeant Wheeler were both at Ghent in 1815, but were there for somewhat different reasons. There is no reason why Ellen Weeton should not have seen the file works of Peter Stubs, since for most of their lives they lived within a few miles of each other. Whether they did or not will remain a secret for some other researcher to explore. I hope that you will feel that you would like to know more about them all and about other people like them; you can do this by reading some of the diaries, which any public library will be able to reserve for you, and by following up some of the suggestions made in the book list. Biography is one of the most absorbing aspects of history, and anyone who wishes to keep their own diary might find at some time the urge to turn it into an autobiography, which is one of the easiest ways to start writing history.

3   George III (born 1738, reigned 1760-1811, died 1820).

4   George IV (born 1762, became Prince Regent 1811, reigned 1820-1830).

1 THE SQUIRE:

Nicholas Blundell

Few characters in eighteenth century literature are better known than the village squire. Nicholas Blundell of Crosby Hall, near Liverpool, was a typical example of the Georgian country gentleman. For 30 years we can follow his activities in his journal, or Great Diurnal: 'A Daly account, wherein I have set down something or other every day that hath happened.' It shows a fascinating picture of the annual round of events, his chief interests and recreations, and the problems that he and his family faced during the first quarter of the century. His friends, tenants and servants come to life again; we know the names of his horses and his dogs. Even the weather which favoured the village of Little Crosby is noted over the years. Not surprisingly we find the repetitive cycle of the farming year, a concern for the well-being of animals and detailed accounts of financial transactions.

He was not a wealthy man; his estate was still burdened by debts going back to the Restoration. He had to make a living and make ends meet by farming, but he still managed to enjoy life. We read of him attending race meetings, coursing hares, going shooting and fishing, placing guineas at stake on the bowling green and in the cock pit, and taking part in all the seasonal festivities of rural England.

His birth is recorded in a manuscript still kept at Crosby Hall called the Great Hodge Podge. The son of William Blundell, he was born in 1669; his grandfather was William Blundell 'the Cavalier', so called because he had fought under Lord Derby's command on the Royalist side in the Civil War. The family had been Lords of the Manor of Little Crosby since the fourteenth century. They were Roman Catholics, who had refused to accept the Elizabethan Settlement of the English Reformation, and had been persecuted for their faith. Since they remained Catholics and did not attend Church of England services they were described as recusants, suffering the penalties which went with that condition. They could not enter the professions or hold public office. They were suspected of treason. During an invasion scare in 1694 William 'the Cavalier' was being hunted by the King's officers as a Jacobite, but since when caught he was thought to be too old and was found to have a game leg, his son William was arrested in his place. This seems to have been the latter's only brush with the law. During the rebellion of the Old Pretender, Nicholas Blundell was suspected: '13 November 1715 — this Hous was twice sirched by some Foot as came from Leverpoole,' so he took refuge in a priest's hole, noting ruefully later, 'I sat in a Streat (narrow) place for a fat Man.' In 1716 he thought it prudent to leave the country for a time, later sending for his wife and family, but there is no evidence that the Blundells were disloyal to the Protestant Succession.

It should not surprise us that the family motto was 'anything for a quiet life' — 'in omnibus requiem quaesivi'. The Blundells kept out of the public eye, although they were on good terms with their neighbour Lord Molyneux of Sefton and were acquaintances of Lord Derby. When Nicholas became the Squire of Crosby Hall on the death of his father one of his first tasks was to find a Catholic wife with a dowry large enough to match his social position. His marriage to Frances, the 17-year-old daughter of Lord Langdale, was an arranged match between a proud and high spirited wife and a husband who wanted money and an heir to succeed him. Frances brought him £2000 and later two daughters, Mary and Frances, who were known as Mally and Fanny, both idolized by their father, but it was his great sorrow that he never had a son.

No doubt the couple grew fond of each other but Frances was a difficult person to live with. Within a year the mother and great-aunt of the new squire had moved out of the Hall for the first time, although Nicholas soon brought them back. His resident chaplain, Father Aldred, later decided to go and live in the village. The rapidity with which servants came and went was another indication of his wife's temper. Nicholas could usually manage her, but whenever his diary spoke of 'She' instead of 'My wife' it indicated trouble: '20 February 1704 — She Quarrelled with me about her not tacking Phisick and my not coming to see and pitty her.' When his daughters came of age his letters insisted that they must be allowed to marry men of their own choice.

We know this from the variety of written records which he kept. An interest in medicine and faith in his own home-made remedies was probably a consequence of his wife's ill-health and his own eye trouble, which he blamed on an ague, perhaps malaria, caught while at school in Flanders. Apart from the usual blood letting, purges,

5   Nicholas Blundell (1669-1737) became Lord of the Manor of Little Crosby on the death of his father, William Blundell, in August 1702.

6   Frances Langdale, wife of Nicholas Blundell: '17 June 1703 I was married to Lord Langdales Doughter [sic] by Mr Slaughter a Clergyman.'

vomits and 'glisters' (enemas) recommended by Doctor Fabius — whose real name was Bean, but who used the Latin form — Nicholas had his own prescription or 'recipe' book with its unusual suggestions. These included steeping his feet in hot whey to cure corns, shaving and blistering his head to ease headache, cutting his ears to aid his eyesight, and from time to time immersing his daughters in the salt waters of the Mersey to cure skin rashes. When the family was abroad he notes: '7 June 1717 — We went into the Bath in the Morning, it is my Wives 13th time and my eleventh.' This was at Chaudefontaine, a Flemish Spa, where the Blundells bathed regularly in the hope that they might beget a son. Not until the final years of his life was Nicholas consoled by a grandson, 'little Master Kitt', whose brother eventually became the new Squire of Crosby.

Most of his life was spent farming. On taking over the estate he had a map made of his lands, using the most accurate measuring instruments he could obtain from Liverpool. Every field, pit and watercourse was distinctly named, and even the trees in his orchard were numbered. Although he generally favoured traditional methods he experimented whenever he heard of something new. In March 1704 his gardener 'Thomas Tickley grafted amany Apple Trees' and later that month he sent his steward Walter Thelwall 'to order my Tennants in the Moorehouses to set Starr upon Fryday next' — star or marram grass being used to bind together sandhills in his fields near the coast. In June 1712 he undertook a more ambitious scheme of marling his land. The spreading of marl, or limy clay, on a field increased its crop yield:

2 June — Some of my Darby Marlers came to see when I would begin of my Marling — 3 June — The Marlers Drink was tuned, I computed how much there was and how many Quarts a day it would be for the Marlers — 5 June — William Ainsworth and I measured over-cross the Little Morehey and the Pick which are to be Maried, we computed how many Carts they would take — 10 June — I computed how many inches there was in a Marl Cart, and what were lost if the Carts were an inch too little — 12 June — I began to Marl. I had two Companys

7   An eighteenth-century pharmaceutical cabinet: Blundell called his store of medicines his 'apothecary shop' and kept a 'Prescription and Recipe Book'.

8   Map of the Manor of Little Crosby: '10 March 1704 I mesured the Oaklands &c: by taking two stasions on each field.'

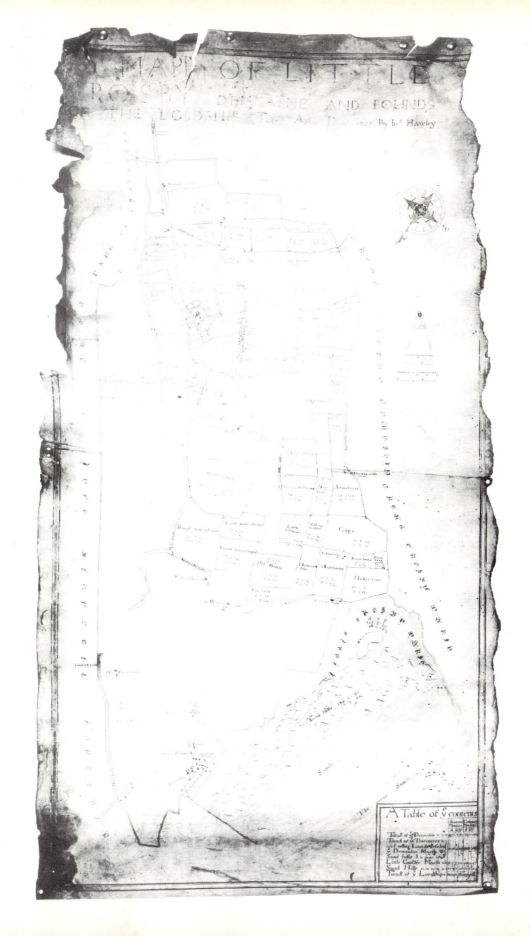

and each Company consisted of three Hewers and four Fillers, there was twelve Carts, four Spreders and one Water Bayly, they got out 754 Load, I was with them soone after three of the Clock in the Morning.

The digging and carting took a month to complete. That this was a considerable achievement for him was signalled by making it the occasion for a celebration:

7 July — I was very busy most of the after-noone shaping Tinsall for the Garland for my New Marl-Pit and after Supper the Women helped to Paste some things for it. I began to teach the 8 Sword Dancers their Dance which they are to Dance at the Flowering of my Marl-Pit — 9 July — All the 14 Marlers had a Particular Dress upon their Heads and carried each of them a Musket or a Gun, the six Garlands were carried by Young Women in Prosestion, the 8 Sword Dancers went along with them to the Marl-pit where they Dansed, the Musick was Gerald Holsold and his Son and Richard Tatlock — 15 July — I Baited a Large Bull in the Bottom of my New Marl-pit, he was never baited before as I know off, yet played to admiration, there was I think 8 or 9 Doggs played the first Bait, I think there was not above two Doggs but what were very ill hurt some Sticked into the Side or Lamed or very ill Brused, I gave a Coller to be played for but no Dogg could get it fairly.

There was cruelty as well as rustic charm in this. The newly dug pit was floored and waterproofed for its future use as a stock pit, but Nicholas was able to find a winter use for it first, before enough water had been diverted in to make it deep enough for fish: '6 December — I skated on my new Marlpit, I hurt my hip ill with a fall on the Ise.' By March 1713 the pit was ready:

I drained the Horsepoole with my Chean Pump and took out of it 62 Carps 4 Tensh and one Bream. William Ainsworth helped me to put 40 of the Carps into my New Marlpit, the rest of the fish was otherways disposed of. William Harrison the Clarke of Sefton was here, I paid him 2d instead of Paist Eggs.

From this we can see that the new pit was to be a Carp stock pit; no doubt eels would be put in to keep the bottom of the pit clean, and some tench — the doctor fish — which were supposed to keep other breeds healthy. Fish was a valuable part of the family diet and it was important to keep the pits clean and free from parasites. The usual method of catching fish for food was by netting or by draining, although in August of that year Squire Blundell went with his chaplain 'Pat. Alldred fishing for shoulers to use as a bait for Pike.' 'Shoulers' or shoalers would be small fish moving in shoals, such as rudd or perch. Eels were kept in 'sniggeries' and caught with snig nets. The stocking of the marl pit had taken place near Easter time, which explains the squire's reference to giving pace eggs, or peace eggs, as an offering to the Sefton clergy.

More variety might be added to the food supply, and more colour to demesne lands near the Hall by the cultivation of a kitchen and nursery garden. There are references to 'Collyflower, Sellery and Red Beet Seed' being sown in the 'Clos-Hedg Garden', which is the hedge close enough to the Hall to dry clothes on, and 'severall Sorts of Salletting in the Kill-Garden' — salad plants in the kiln or kitchen garden. Flowers and nursery seedlings were grown in a flower knot which he made in front of the dining room window. One of Dutch William's preferences which he had brought with him to England in 1688 was a liking for tulips, and no patriotic English garden was without them:

I put some good old Muck to five of my best Flower Beds in the Knot and to my Bed of Forrain Tulops and to one Bed in the Nursery of Flowers. I set about 1500 Tulop Roots and Chives in the Nursery.' This was in July 1720, 'very unconstant Weather some days very hot but generally more rain than we could wish for our Harvest.

This last reminds us that Squire Blundell was a farmer, and that his activities were predictable — winter ditching would always be followed by ploughing and sowing, turf and timber would be cut and stacked, hay-making would depend upon the summer weather and the harvest home would tell of a good or bad year. At all times there would be the need to manage his livestock; rearing, buying, selling and slaughtering would go on in company with his neighbours and with the labour available in the roadside village outside his gates. The same seasonal festivities and ceremonies would be repeated. This is how the majority of eighteenth century people spent their lives. Their squire shared in their work, pleasures and pastimes, and if he was like Nicholas Blundell

he would be thought a true gentleman if he lent them his greyhounds for coursing hares, his nets for fishing, and his coach or cart for accidents and burials. When they were ill they could expect a visit or a medicine which he might even prescribe and make up himself, and in the appropriate season he might join them in their cottages for pancakes and Christmas pudding.

He could be a strict employer when he chose: '8 June 1708 — I and Thelwall went with William Weedon the Cunstable to Richard Ainsworths and brought home in a Cart some Booords Iron Etc: as he had stolen from me (Ainsworth was his ploughman at Crosby) — 4 August — I Bowled at Ince Green with old Robert Bootle, Gill the Exciseman came to the Aile-hous whilst we were drinking. I cut Mallys hair off, My Wife and Mary Howerd cut off mine. Richard Ainsworth desired to know whether I would pardon him before the Assizes, I told him noe — 19 August — I dined at my Lodgings with Mr Roughley and one or two more

9 Coursing: '26 December 1709 Walter Thelwall, John Hunt etc. went a coursing with me, we started about 8 Hars in I think less than two Hours time.'

of the Grand Jury — 20 August — Richard Ainsworth was found guilty of Robery — 21 August — Richard Ainsworth and two others were burned in the hand.' He occasionally took the law into his own hands: '28 October 1728 — I had seaven Lads of this Town beaton at my Gate-Hous with a Sterrop-Leather, some by their fathers, others by their Masters for Stealing my Apples and for other Peevish tricks.'

For the most part Squire Blundell was a good friend, a diligent farmer and a cheerful neighbour. There was no October ploughing at Crosby, probably because the low lying land was never dry enough, and the farming year there began with the Michaelmas Fair on Goose Feast Monday, a time for hiring labour and meeting friends. Livestock was brought into winter housing near the Hall and the field boundaries for the new year marked by 'meer-stones', a surviving feudal practice. Blundell went coursing in winter — once noting that his hounds met those of Lord Molyneux behind Crosby School after which the two men had dinner at the Hall. They sometimes went hunting together and were often together at local race meetings, which were organized on Crosby sands, when a track was marked out and a two lap distance agreed, which seems to have been nearly four miles. The Blundell family had an ancient responsibility here, for the course started and finished on their land, and in August 1718 the Squire notes: 'I went to Crosby Marsh and ordered where the Distance Post should stand and saw them fixing the Chear,' which was the start.

The twelve days of Christmas were kept with great enjoyment. Gifts were made to cottagers as well as to yeomen and gentry. There was always a party at the Hall: '28 December 1711 — Robert Rimer and his Wife brought me both Fish and Fowl. We had a merry night, Tatlock played here of his Pipes and Fiddle, there was pritty throng Carding, one Company played at 6d. p Cut

till after Nine next Morning.' On Twelfth Night 1714 Blundell notes: 'Mr. Plumb, Doctor Lancaster I & C: was at Mrs Anns Cocking, there were Three Battles, but I onely stayed two of them. Tatlock was here, we had a Merry-Night and Fier'd the Gunns of my Ship.'

This last was a reference to a model man o' war which stood in the entrance hall at Crosby, perhaps a reminder of the war with France and of its successful outcome in that year. The 'Cocking' was cock-fighting which took place on every holiday, usually at Mrs Ann Rothwell's house at Four Lane Ends. Blundell was a devotee of the sport, which was an occasion for heavy gambling. In February 1713 he helped to build a cock-fighting arena for a great contest, 'eather Battle Victory or Battle Royall upon Easter Munday.' William Ainsworth was sent to Blackburn Fair to buy a good fighting cock which was put on a special diet; others were bought, penned and spurred for practice. Blundell took numerous bets and placed money on behalf of friends, his 'Ditton Cock Clumsy' being the favourite to win. On the great day his cocks won two battles and he was so excited that he failed to return home in time to say farewell to departing visitors.

Apart from bacon feasts on 'Collop Monday' and pancakes on Shrove Tuesday the first three months after Christmas were for hedging, ditching and draining. Cleaning out or 'Slutching' water courses was vital at Crosby. Once the ground had hardened coal was usually brought from the coal-pit on the estate. When it snowed there was a chance to trace and snare rabbits, and in better weather mole-traps were set. Like every countryman the Squire welcomed the Spring, noted his first cuckoo and swallow, sent his eggs for sale to Liverpool and began Spring sowing. He saw that his windmill — an experimental one with six sails — was 'whisked and Lickered about', or lubricated with lard and tried out. In May came seeding and sheep-shearing, his beef cattle were sold at Wigan Fair, and he negotiated with his farming friends in bowling matches at Ince Blundell. These last were clearly social and business occasions attended by gentry, clergy and tenants. The summer months brought the hardest work, but there was still the odd day's pleasure in shooting, fishing or racing. In July 1704 Blundell noted: 'I Lead Turf with Boon Carts', a reference to tenants still paying rent in a medieval way by services — in this case by cutting cartloads of turf for the Squire. Harvest Home was the high point of the year, with the ceremony of 'cutting the neck' or reaping the last field in the first week in September. So the years passed at Crosby Hall, with the unusual event always recorded in the Squire's notebook: 'Thos Jackson came home after being a prisoner in France'; 'My greyhound Hector took a live partridge and ran with it in his mouth'; 'Mr Alldred said Mass at West Lane House — I served him — this was the first Catholick Chapel built in England since the Reformation'; 'I mixed some ingredients to make Aqua Coelestes' from smuggled brandy, crab apples, lemon and sugar mixed to his own recipe.

But more than most men of his time Nicholas Blundell travelled a good deal on business in Derbyshire and Yorkshire, and he had spent months abroad in the Netherlands as a Catholic refugee. In January 1716 he rode his mare Ginny to London and met several other Catholic gentry there, took a room with a good lock on the door and began to learn French. When his wife and family joined him in Belgium they treated the exile as a holiday and did much sight-seeing. Nicholas records seeing Peter the Great — 'the Zar of Muscovy' — in Liège. He visited the Spas and delighted acquaintances with his card tricks and 'Ledgerdemesne'. At the Convent of the Poor Clares at Gravelines he met his great-aunt and his two sisters, who had been refugees in an earlier age. Nicholas and his wife left their two daughters at the Convent to complete their education, eventually returning to bring them home in 1723. Meanwhile the Jacobite danger had passed and Squire Blundell and his wife made their way back to Crosby after sampling the delights of London which they had not visited since they were married.

'The Great Diurnal of Nicholas Blundell' ends in 1728 nine years before his death. Failing eyesight and other duties had caused its abandonment. Anxious to set his affairs in order, for he was 60 years old, Nicholas was drawing up a fresh Tenants' book for the new squire of Crosby. He was succeeded by the husband of his younger daughter Fanny, and by her third son Nicholas who assumed the name Blundell in 1772, with the arms of Blundell of Crosby, and continued the family succession.

10 A champion cock: 'I went to Ormskirk Cocking, it being the second days fighting for a Plate. Lost and Spent 8s.0d.'

2 THE SURGEON:

Richard Kay

Most people have heard of John Kay of Bury, the inventor of the flying shuttle. Few know of his relative, Doctor Richard Kay of Baldingstone, whose diary is one of the authentic records of general medical training and practice at that time. The name Kay was so common in Lancashire that it was usual to add the place of residence to the surname. Baldingstone was a country house two miles to the north of Bury. Doctor Robert Kay had inherited it from his father Richard Kay, and was living there when his son Richard was born in 1716. The boy's mother Elizabeth was the daughter of Samuel Taylor, a Nonconformist minister of Moston, near Manchester. The family

attended Silver Street Chapel in Bury built by their uncle, another Richard Kay, who had made his money as a linen merchant before setting up as a country gentleman.

Our Richard Kay went to the local village school until he was nearly 14. Then his father persuaded him to leave and join him in the surgery as his assistant. It was expected that the boy would serve as an apprentice and qualify as a doctor as his father had done before him. There was room for another doctor in the family, for the practice

11 Doctor Kay would have kept the ingredients for his medicines in a box of drawers like this.

was spread over an area radiating for 10 or 15 miles around Bury, and called for much hard and difficult riding across the moor and moss. Doctor Kay prescribed and prepared his own medicines, and often performed operations within the homes of his patients. He expected his son to look after the surgery during his absence, and to be prepared to treat anyone who came to 'the shop'. Doctor Kay passed on knowledge and advice to his son whenever he could. Another relative, Doctor Samuel Kay of Manchester, encouraged young Richard to study hard and qualify as a surgeon.

Richard was not so sure; he was a deeply religious boy who thought seriously about a career in the Presbyterian Church. He kept a notebook in which he recorded all the sermons, lectures and prayer meetings which he attended at Bury Chapel. Visiting preachers would often be entertained at Baldingstone so he was well used to such company. His diary contains many entries listed simply as 'closet duties', which was his description for sessions of private prayer and meditation. Nevertheless we can see from it that he divided his time after leaving school between the Surgery, the Chapel and the general farming and gardening work of a country doctor's estate.

Nonconformist behaviour then was not so strict as it later became in Victorian times. Although he spent his Sundays listening to sermons he seldom missed a visit to any of the local Fairs. When there was a race meeting at Kersal Moor he was almost sure to be there. His diary entry usually concludes with a sentence indicating how he reflected upon his behaviour during the day, and on these occasions he might write: 'Lord ever keep me in good and sober company, and guard against mad frolics.'

In the spring and summer of 1737 it is clear that he was becoming dissatisfied with his lack of a proper profession. After working with carpenters at Baldingstone and felling timber, not to mention being roundly cursed by a passing carrier, he wrote that these activities were for persons 'of meaner extract and education than myself'. In October he was out coursing rabbits when he was called home to set a boy's thigh bone and to dress the head wound of another boy who had fallen into a stone-pit. Later in the same month he was out with his father visiting fracture cases, and then he took the place of the Baldingstone schoolmaster for a day when Mr Crompton was away. In November he was setting fruit trees. On November the Fifth he went to the annual Thanksgiving sermon for the country's deliverance from the Gunpowder Plot, and a week later he wrote that he deputized for his father in the surgery attending to bruises and broken bones. It was about this time that he had a dream that he ought to make medicine his career: 'extraordinary dreams in extraordinary circumstances ought not to pass regardless by us.'

From the beginning of 1738 he seems, like many other sons, to have settled for his father's profession. He still enjoyed himself, going crossbow shooting, watching bowling matches and visiting the races; he still stood in for Mr Crompton at the school or helped bring home the harvest, but more and more medical details are creeping into his notebooks. He writes about the dangers of horse traffic passing on narrow roads, of the health benefits of the liquorice roots that he bought at Pontefract, and of the need for finding a quick remedy for toothache. He suffered from this himself: 'O my tooth, my tooth, no remedy takes effect' he wrote in February 1739, after coming home from a lecture on anatomy. By this time he was studying medicine and theology alternately. In the summer of that year he visited the spa of Buxton to take the waters, and wrote home that he and his cousin Sam

Taylor were 'having a deal of good and profitable discourse with the local clergy'.

The apprentice-doctor was learning his trade at no little risk to his patients. By September 1740 he was mixing his own medicines; after giving an overdose to a man who lived too far away for the mistake to be corrected he wrote: 'I am no little uneasy about it but I hope it will be a means to make me very careful for the future.' He was treating himself for a tumour of the gum by rubbing liquid laudanum into his cheeks. What effect this had he does not say, but it was a well known way of drugging babies to sleep about a century later with the Victorians. We cannot be sure what Richard meant when he wrote that he was treating 'strumous and scrofulous disorders' but there can be no doubt about the extremely painful and often fatal consequences of this rough and ready medication, disguised as it was in pompous Latin terminology. In April 1740 he stayed the night with his cousin Joshua Taylor:

In the evening Cousin Joshua was trubled with sickness, occasioned as was supposed by being too long in the Cold Evening upon the Bowling Green and then coming to a hot fire . . . they sent for Doctor Watson, who ordered him to be bled, and prescribed for him a vomit and a sweat successively.

12 **A respectable game for centuries, in the eighteenth century bowls became associated with wagers and ale houses.**

Had the unfortunate Joshua not recovered quickly he would have been 'blistered' as well.

By this time Richard was studying the effects of smallpox and attending lecture courses, which were being paid for by his cousin Samuel Kay, who was a physician in Manchester. At Baldingstone he was planting trees in his new walled garden and collecting money for the school. This latter duty he did not much like, since it was a condition in a legacy of 50 pounds left to the school by James Lancaster of Middleton, who stipulated that another 50 should be raised by public collection. He had no holiday in the following year, but he went to Liverpool to see the shipping there, following the outbreak of war with France and Spain. In February 1742 he 'took a walk in the afternoon to Bury, with great numbers beside, to see a Football match between town and country. Lord may I not regard iniquity in my heart'.

He was now fairly confident of his own powers of diagnosis: '28 April. Visiting a patient near Heywood under a scrofulous disorder in his ankle bones, I advised him to an amputation or taking off of his leg which he complied to.' Sometimes there was a crowd of patients to deal with: 'I waited on my father in the shop — we had a broken arm, a broken thigh, a tumour in the leg, a tumour in the shoulder and a thigh muscle severed at the kneecap.' He was occasionally very depressed by the frightening nature of his work, and was convinced that he was himself suffering from many of the ailments which he saw. From time to time he thought that his eyesight was failing.

In the summer of 1742 he cheered himself up by going on holiday to the Lake District with his cousin Samuel Taylor, who had to make a business trip to linen check merchants in Whitehaven. It is characteristic of the eighteenth century traveller that he noted a visit 'to Mr Rothram's

celebrated Orrery at Kendal' but never once commented on the natural beauty of the landscape through which they passed, although they rode on horseback through Kendal, Ambleside and Keswick, returning by a different route through Carlisle, Penrith and Shap. In the following summer of 1743, he went to Manchester lectures on 'Dioptics and Katoptics', visited Bolton Fair, and saw the Swedish giant 'eight feet tall' before attending a Thanksgiving service at Bury Chapel for the Royal victory at Dettingen.

August of that year was a turning point in his life. He was 27 years old when his kinsman Samuel Kay put forward the fee of 24 guineas needed for him to train as a surgeon at Guy's Hospital. With a signed certificate of good character he set out on a hired horse to ride to London, to become a pupil to Mr Benjamin Stead, apothecary at Guy's and supervisor of apprentices. Accompanied by several friends for the first day he eventually rode with Edward Sparrow, a young apothecary returning to London after visiting friends in Lancashire. The journey took five days. Once

there Richard found that he was one of three pupils attached to Mr Stead for an intensive course of lectures and attendance at operations. He decided not to record these in detail in his diary, although he did send his father a journal of his work.

While in London he determined not to miss the chance to see the sights. These included the Lord Mayor's Show, a visit to Bedlam, to St James's 'to see the Quality go to the Ball', and the public hanging of five men and a woman on Kennington Common. Sometimes he went to Covent Garden or Drury Lane to see the play. 'This day I saw the war proclaimed against the French in the City' he wrote, and, in July 1744, 'I saw Commodore Anson's Treasure pass through the City, there were 32 waggons loaded with silver and gold. Lord prosper our arms.' He needed some relief of this sort: 'seeing little in these

19

hospitals but affliction and death I find it necessary for me now and then to seek out some diversion'. For Richard this meant attendance at religious meetings — on one Sunday in November he listened to five different kinds of services, and at other times he went to Mass at Popish celebrations, or to Moor Fields to listen to the Field Preacher John Wesley. He would never have dared to do this at home, but in London he could please himself.

In August 1744 the apprenticeship was over. Mr Sharp, the surgeon at Guy's, signed his Certificate and he collected his case of new surgical instruments. There seem to have been the usual end-of-term 'student rags': 'I boxed one of the pupils today — the first person that I ever struck in my life — he charged me publicly tho' in jest with debauchery of which I was innocent.' Now aged 28, Doctor Richard Kay, Surgeon, rode back home in a leisurely tour through Windsor, Oxford, pausing at Blenheim Palace, and on through Stratford to Lichfield. He went through the Peak District into Lancashire, there to be met by friends with much rejoicing and escorted back to Baldingstone.

From then on he shared the practice with his father. They travelled everywhere on horseback, sometimes covering remark-

14 **The case of surgical instruments given to a medical student after completing his course at Guy's Hospital.**

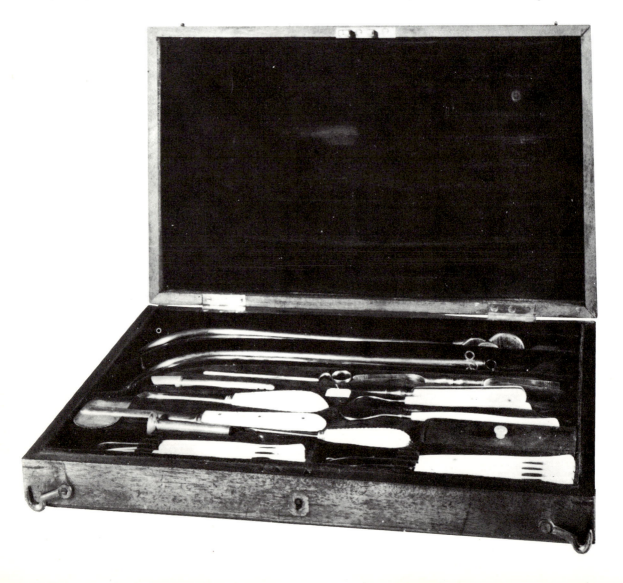

able distances. On one occasion his father estimated that he had ridden between 15 and 16 hundred miles in treating one patient over the years. In November 1745 Richard had just amputated a woman's leg when he heard that the Jacobite rebels were approaching the district. The local gentry hid their valuables and sent away their horses. Friends from Manchester and Uncle and Aunt Taylor from Moston sought shelter at Baldingstone.

Within a few days the rebels were retreating back along the road they had come. 'December 10. Having never seen the Rebels or any in Highland dress I set out this morning on foot with some other friends to see them march on the road from Manchester to Wigan.' Three days later he went to see the Duke of Cumberland's

15 'November 26 We hear this evening a serjeant with one drummer belonging to the Pretender's service are come to Manchester today and have enlisted several into their service.'

army passing through in pursuit — 'it gives abundance of joy to good people to all true Protestants to see such a number of fine forces.' He saw Mr Chandler, an apprentice surgeon whom he had known at Guy's, following Cumberland's army. Meanwhile the family went back to work. In April 1746 he spent an evening rejoicing with friends at the news of Culloden. The Jacobites had recruited about 30 soldiers in Manchester, and those who were caught were brought back and beheaded. Two of them were Deacon and Siddall, whose heads were fixed upon the Manchester Exchange —

this was a sombre reminder for Lancashire Jacobites, for Siddall's father had suffered the same shameful fate in 1715 as a supporter of the Old Pretender. At the end of October Richard Kay noted that he had spent the evening at a ball at the Manchester Exchange in rejoicing for the deliverance of the Protestant cause.

By this time Richard had become the more active of the partners in the family business. He might ride 30 miles in a single round, and he had some nasty experiences. His worst was in December 1748 when he was returning by night from a visit in Rossendale. In the pitch darkness his horse was being led across a stone bridge by a local man when it fell over the parapet with the doctor in the saddle and dropped 20 feet into the water. By divine intervention, or so it seemed to his friends, neither horse nor rider was injured.

It was not surprising that with trials like this Doctor Kay welcomed an occasional day's holiday. He went back to Buxton again, and later visited Chatsworth. He was as assiduous as ever in his religious duties, but was dismayed at the way in which music was intruding in church services: 'I was asked last week to subscribe to an instrument called a bassoon, to be played upon in Bury Church — it seems to me to be a merry way of getting to Heaven.' Nor did he much like the popularity of the new organ at Manchester old church which he was invited to listen to in November 1747. These were to him High Church practices and more examples of the 'Church Bigotry' of which he often complained. He never ceased to thank God for the Hanoverian Succession which had saved England from 'Popish slavery and vain idolatory'.

Doctor Richard Kay's skill as a surgeon was by this time more than locally recognized, but in reading the notes of his operations we must still be horrified at the incredible pain which patients had to suffer in those pre-anaesthetic days. Skill and speed with a sharp knife was everything. A couple of swift sweeps with blood spurting everywhere and the job was done. One case will suffice. At Christmas 1748 he took off the cancerous right breast of Mrs Driver of Crawshaw Booth. During the following June he 'dissected from her five hundred different schirrous knots or young cancers' with further dissections around her armpit and neck a month later. In September he

16 **The knife and saw used in an amputation.**

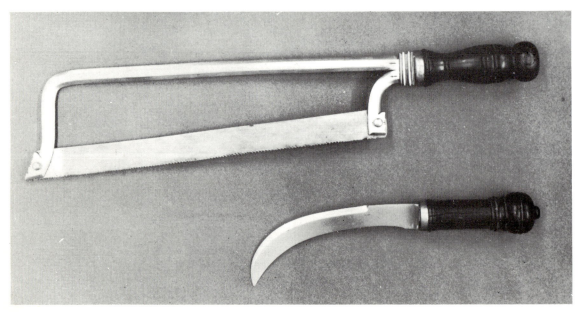

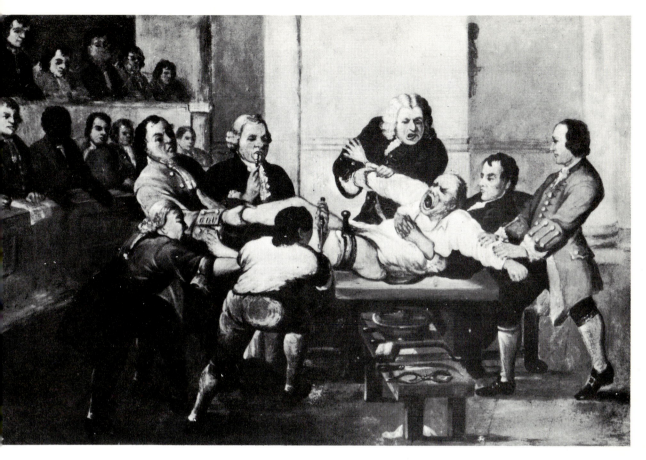

17 **How best to amputate a limb: this was a considerable advance from the practices of the barber-surgeons.**

'took from her right side three different cancers about the size each of a hen's egg' and cut four or five more from the same wound in October. Mrs Driver lived until February 1750, when Richard attended her funeral at Goodshaw Church.

By this time, although he did not know it, he was facing death himself. In February 1750 we find the following entry in his diary: 'This fever with small eruptions, or small red freckles, is like unto common flea bites.' He called it the spotted fever, but from modern medical knowledge we recognize this as the outbreak of typhus, a disease as deadly as the plague in eighteenth century England. The diary entries stop in July 1750. Richard's brother in law, Joseph Baron, died from the epidemic before this date. By the end of the year his father was dead. Carrying on the practice alone was a great strain. We know that Richard Kay was a strong man; he tells us that he was six feet two inches high and 210 pounds in weight, but it is likely that he was becoming more prone to the disease himself as the number of cases multiplied. In October 1751 Richard himself, his sister Elizabeth and his mother all died within days of each other. Their friend Thomas Braddock preached a funeral sermon for them at Bury Chapel, and they were buried in what is now the chapel yard of Bank Street Unitarian Chapel, Bury. Doctor Richard Kay, Surgeon, of Baldingstone, a profoundly loyal Protestant Dissenter, was 35 years old.

23

3 THE PRINCESS:
Betty Berkeley

The name 'Anspach Place', incised on the Georgian facade of a house built into the medieval walls of Southampton, offers a riddle for visitors to the modern city and provides a starting point for the story of Betty Berkeley. About two hundred years ago the town revived when the Prince of Wales, father of the future George III, went there in 1750 for the sea bathing. Where the Prince led, the nobility and gentry followed:

18 **Betty Berkeley, Lady Craven. A portrait by George Romney in 1778.**

enterprising local speculators laid out the Spa Gardens and erected Baths and Assembly Rooms close to the West Quay. One of the houses built for this royal retinue was later occupied by Elizabeth, Baroness Craven, afterwards Margravine of Anspach and Bayreuth and Princess Berkeley of the Holy Roman Empire.

Betty Berkeley was both witty and attractive; she was painted by Gainsborough, Reynolds and Romney; she corresponded with Doctor Johnson, Garrick and Horace Walpole. Yet in an age remembered both in Britain and France for women of remarkable intellect and beauty she hardly seems to have been noticed. Why was this? She was too young to belong to the world of Lady Mary Wortley Montagu and Mrs Vesey — the learned ladies known as 'Bluestockings' — and perhaps too old by the time the Prince Regent was leading fashionable society in the elegant candlelight of Carlton House. Her social lifetime matches most nearly the reign of George III, who, from his residences at Kew and Windsor, imposed an interlude of propriety which his plain and worthy Queen Charlotte formalized into a system of stiff etiquette. However much she tried, the Princess Berkeley was not received at Court because she was not thought respectable.

This had not always been so. Born in 1750 at Charborough, Dorset, she was the youngest daughter of the fourth Earl of

Berkeley, and was presented at Court on her sixteenth birthday, 'to be received by the world, cherished by relations and courted by men'. Her father died five years after she was born; her mother never liked her. Lady Berkeley had been hoping for a boy and when the girl was born she was wrapped in a flannel blanket and put by on a chair to die. A visitor who called noticed the brightness of her eyes, pronounced her full of life, and sent out immediately for a wet nurse. So Betty was saved. She was consigned to the care of a Swiss governess who brought her up most properly to be able to sing and dance and speak fluent French.

At 14, with her soft, auburn hair and her hazel eyes, she went to her first ball. Two years later she was married to William Craven, later the sixth Baron Craven, who took her away to his estate at Benham Valence, Newbury, where they had seven children in 13 years. Then the husband gave his wife an allowance of £1500 a year and told her to go her own way out of his life forever. At least this is what her *Memoires* relate, although written at the age of 76, by an old lady trying to recapture her life and loves.

Of course it cannot have been exactly like that. Dedicated to the Duke of York, her *Memoires* gave no inkling that there was anything improper about her behaviour. On the other hand a reader of the *Town and Country Magazine* or the *Jockey Club* gossip columns would immediately consign her to the company of professional courtesans. The truth must lie somewhere between these extremes. For years she had a fascinating beauty, a sparkling wit and a fluent pen, which made her enemies as well as friends. In the end she was seen to be neither a great writer nor a good woman. Her earlier indiscretions might have been forgotten, but her ruthless pursuit and conquest of the effeminate Margrave of Anspach as a means to wealth and social

19 Benham Valence, Newbury, where Lady Betty lived for 13 years after her marriage, and to which she returned as Margravine of Anspach.

status, in which she spurned his wife and drove off his French mistress, was outrageous even when judged by the dissipated standards of those days.

Of her first husband she says that he was fond and stupid while she was beautiful and clever. In that he was determined to marry her, and take her away from Court before she found a place in it, he may only have encouraged her to attract a circle of followers to Benham. By 1773 her affairs were public enough to be reported in the *Morning Chronicle*. It was said that Lord Craven had established for himself that there was a liaison between his wife and the French ambassador to the Court of St James's, the Duc de Guines, and that he had challenged the man to a duel. The Duc de Guines declined to accept so long as he remained in his official position, but he does not seem to have been the only admirer of Lady Betty at this time.

She otherwise amused herself by writing and translating — songs, charades, epilogues and sonnets were composed between continual correspondence with literary figures — and in 1780 one of her plays, 'The Miniature Picture', performed originally at Newbury Town Hall for the benefit of the poor, was put on for a few nights at Drury Lane. 'Perdita' Robinson, the favourite of the Prince of Wales, had a part in this and Sheridan wrote the prologue. It was reported that 'she went to it herself on the second night, in form, sat in the middle of the front row of the stage box, much dressed in a profusion of white bugles and plumes, to receive the public homage due to her sex and loveliness . . . it was amazing to see a young woman so entirely possess herself.' Some years later her pantomime version of 'Puss in Boots' was published. When in London she usually lived in Hill Street, but Lord Craven had formed the habit of giving her a lottery ticket each year, and with money from a win she bought land at Fulham on the Thames and built a small house there, which she named Craven Cottage.

In 1783 she left England with her favourite son Keppel, after agreeing with Lord Craven to return the boy on his eighth birthday, so long as her other children were allowed to write to her. Neither side kept this bargain. Henceforth her husband ignored her; she complained that 'his aversion for me is so much increased, instead of being diminished' when writing from Florence in 1785, and there was to be no reconciliation. She left her son to be educated in Paris while she lived in Versailles. This was where she first met the Margrave of Anspach. After leaving Paris she toured for three years through the capitals of Europe and Asia in the company of Henry Vernon, a distant relation of the famous Admiral.

The account which she later published

shows that she had travelled further than any other Englishwoman of her day. From Vienna she went to Cracow and Warsaw, where King Stanislaus II sought to please her by ordering that everything should be cooked 'a l'Anglaise', that is, covered with melted butter. Lady Betty did not tell him that all the best cooks in England were French. She thought it amusing that Polish girls of good family were obliged to wear little bells on the front and back of their dresses, so that their parents might know where they were.

From there she went to St Petersburg, to be received by the Empress Catherine the Great at the Hermitage, an odd name, she thought, for so magnificent a palace. She approved of the practice of setting apart separate houses for foreigners of distinction, by which the Empress hoped to attract western experts to Russia, and appreciated the evening concerts, French plays and Italian operas which entertained and educated the Russian nobility. Then she went to Moscow, which she did not like, and on through Tartary to Sevastopol to catch a frigate for Constantinople.

There she was met by the French Ambassador, the Duc de Choiseul, who was her host, despite protests from the English community that she should have favoured them. She records seeing the Sultan sitting on a silver sofa, with his beard dyed black so that he might be recognized from a distance, surrounded by his guard of janissaries. Two of these warriors were detailed as her escort in her trips round the city. Turkish women she described as 'walking mummies', so wrapped up were they, but she found it diverting that their husbands would not enter the harem if the slippers of a visiting lady were placed outside — how easy, she said, for another man to dress in veils and carry a pair of lady's slippers for a secret assignation!

On her way home she stopped in Greece to visit the sites of antiquity, and then

21 The Sultan's audience chamber. 'They break-fasted with the Empress of Russia, they dined with the Grand Signior and supped with the Great Mogul' (Horace Walpole's description of her Grand Tour).

went by Varna and Bucharest to Vienna. Here she persuaded old Prince Kaunitz to introduce her to the Margravine of Anspach. So she met the wife of the man who had visited her so frequently at Versailles. Lady Betty was not impressed: 'naturally fair, sickness gave her the appearance of a faded lily when it begins to assume a yellow hue. With the best intentions she had not the power to give expression to a feeling.'

Christian Frederick Charles Alexander, Margrave of Brandenburg, Anspach and Bayreuth, Duke of Prussia and Count of Sayn, was a nephew both of Frederick the Great of Prussia and of Caroline of Anspach, Queen of England and wife of George II. This absolute prince, who throughout his life was a slave to beauty, ruled a tiny state within the Empire, the toy principalities of Anspach and Bayreuth — in modern Bavaria — famous for their baroque architecture and operatic tradition. Before

Lady Betty left Paris she had ensured that the Margrave would not forget her. Her candid friend Horace Walpole wrote: 'She has I fear been *infinamente* indiscreet, but what is that to you or me, she is very pretty, has parts, and is good natured to the greatest degree.'

Lady Betty remained in England only for a short time, staying with her mother, then Lady Nugent, and later with her brother George in Sussex. She wrote letters to noble lords in the hope that they might influence the King to give the Margrave an English title, but her pleading was unsuccessful, and so in the winter of 1786 she set out for Germany again. This time she stayed for five years. She found the French actress, Mademoiselle Clairon, installed at Anspach as the royal mistress, and described by the Margrave as 'sa Maman'. Betty said that she had come to be his adopted sister! English journalists told the tale to their readers: 'What chance had a mistress of many years standing, and who was in her fifty first year, against a new charmer of seven and thirty summers?' Lady Betty herself gave another explanation: 'I made my appearance — it was impossible for her to be blind to the sincere regard which the Margrave had for me. Her talents were great as an actress, but her affectation of virtue was truly ridiculous. She was the greatest liar that ever existed.' After a scene which did credit to the great traditions of French tragedy Mademoiselle departed, leaving the stage to her rival.

From either Anspach or Triesdorf news arrived in England of her activities. 'I am teaching the Franconians some English comforts. I have but little time to myself between the Margrave and his wife. I ride out all day and I play in the evening, and if they leave me a moment I am busy making an English farm and garden.' She thought the court life too formal, so formed a court orchestra and a literary club. She wrote plays for the royal theatre and persuaded members of the court to act in them. Her position at Anspach may have been questionable but several English lords and ladies found time to visit her. In later years she wrote: 'at Anspach I amused myself innocently and educated my child.'

She seems to have done more than this. In 1790 she accompanied the Margrave on a visit to Frederick William II in Berlin, where they discussed plans for surrendering his principalities to Prussia. Lady Betty suggested that a financial arrangement in favour of the Margrave would be more permanent than a mere pact of friendship

22 **Her Majesty Queen Charlotte, with her children in the background.**

between two members of the House of Brandenburg. The Prussian Grand Duchess Von Voss recorded that 'it passes understanding that such a person is received at this court. She converses only with the Margrave, who seems to be bewitched by her.'

Lady Betty got her way. In March, 1791, the Margravine died and she at once decided to return with the Margrave to England — as the press put it — 'The Margrave, all goodness, meekness and resignation; the Lady all eyes, fire and fury against the beastly Germans who accused her of leading their gentle sovereign out of his senses and out of their dominions.' Not received in London they left again for Lisbon, where news came that Lord Craven had died, so they were married in the chapel of the British Embassy with all the English naval officers attending as witnesses. Horace Walpole wrote: 'Lady Craven received the news of her husband's death on a Friday, went into weeds on Saturday, and into white satin and many diamonds on Sunday, and in that vestal attire was married to the Margrave of Anspach. The bride excused herself for having so few diamonds; they had been the late Margravine's, but she is to have many more and will soon set out for England.'

This time, she thought, they would not be excluded, but she immediately found a letter from her children saying that out of respect for their late father they would not see her, and a letter from the Queen saying that she would not be received at Court. The Margrave's late subjects were informed that they were from 1791 subjects of the King of Prussia. In 1793 the German Emperor conferred a title on Lady Betty as Princess Berkeley of the Holy Roman Empire. Even this did not compel George III, Queen Charlotte and the Royal Princesses to remove their ban, and Betty was told that her German title of Princess would not be recognized in England, where she would continue to be addressed as the Margravine of Anspach.

By this time she did not care. She would disregard the social veto of her royal relation, the Queen. If she could not go to Court then the Court must be made to come to her. Her new residence at Brandenburg House, Hammersmith, soon became the talk of the town and the centre of the gay set. She even had *Gentlemen* of the Bedchamber. The Prince of Wales and his royal brothers attended concerts and masked balls there — £18,000 was spent on plate, with a gold service for the Prince himself — a private theatre was built at which the Margravine appeared as author, producer and director. Naturally she gave herself all the best parts, with her faithful son Keppel often playing the male lead. She was Viola to his Sebastian in 'Twelfth Night'. The theatre went out of fashion in the dark days of 1797 and the Margrave bought back Benham Valence, so that she might re-establish her position in Berkshire. Once there she presented new colours to the local Volunteers and wrote a song for them, which she sang at a reception in the New-bury Town Hall. She was in Paris after the Peace of Amiens and was 'cut' by Napoleon after forcing her attentions on him by asking for a personal flag of safe conduct home.

By this time she was over 50 and her good looks were gone: 'it would be tedious and too trivial for me to recite the variety of ways by which I endeavoured to divert the Margrave's attention from disagreeable things.' In 1806 he died, and his wife at once set out for Anspach to recover what still belonged to him, while Keppel was dispatched to the King of Prussia to claim a pension. Nothing seems to have come of either of these ventures, but at least she was the owner of properties worth £150,000 and accepted in that circle around the Prince of Wales and Mrs Fitzherbert as they moved between London and the fashionable resorts. This was when she lived in Southampton, near the present 'Royal Standard' inn. The Brandenburg House theatre flourished again for a few years, but it is difficult now to regard Her Serene Highness as anything more than a royal place-seeker. Her son Keppel was in Italy with his friend Sir William Gell, attending the unfortunate Princess of Wales as her chamberlains. Before Waterloo, Lady Betty could be found at Ghent, consoling the wretched but resilient Louis XVIII.

She had visited Italy with Prince Kaunitz years ago, and now decided to turn her back on England and seek refuge in Naples. The King, Ferdinand IV, was a widower who gave her a warm welcome and a villa overlooking the bay. She did not find him attractive: 'His nose was immoderately long. His features were coarse and harsh; he reminded me of a rustic, elevated by some accident to the crown.' Nor did she much like some of his habits: 'the King never missed a shot, and would cut up the animals after they were killed with all the skill of a butcher.' However, she was unlikely to be welcomed home by George IV when her son was giving evidence for the defence at the trial of Queen Caroline. 'The Queen of Indiscretions', as she was called, later became the last inhabitant of Brandenburg House.

In 1825 Lady Betty returned to England for the last time, to see a monument erected at Benham Valence to the memory of the Margrave, and then went back to Naples with her son. Louis XVIII, whom she met again, suggested that she should write her *Memoires,* which were attacked in London after her death as 'a tissue of egotism and vanity'. For several years she had the Duchess of Devonshire as a friend in Naples, but a final description of her comes from the biographer of Lady Blessington, who had a pen as vitriolic as her own: 'a desiccated, antiquated piece of mortality, remarkable for vivacity, realizing the idea of a galvanized Egyptian Mummy.'

She died in Naples in 1828 and was buried in the English cemetery there as was her son Keppel, years later, and his friend the archaeologist, Sir William Gell. She was a typical example of the fast set of Georgian England: at her best an amiable beauty and a tolerant hostess, and at her worst a selfish, ostentatious adventuress. The *Jockey Club* had once called her 'a democrat in love, complaisant to the canaille,' but this is too spiteful when she is placed in the setting of her age. Horace Walpole had a final, kind few words: 'How proud I should be to register a noble authoress of my own country, who has travelled over more regions and farther than any female in print . . . and never has been an enemy but to herself.'

23 **Naples in the eighteenth century.**

4 THE SMUGGLER:
Harry Carter

The steep and rocky coastline of south west Cornwall can be a remote and dangerous place even today. Two hundred years ago it was an unknown and inaccessible part of England, whose inhabitants spoke a language better understood by the Welsh and Bretons of France than by their own countrymen. Wild and half civilized, the Cornishmen lived in villages of four or five cottages, and farmed the land, worked the tin mines and went to sea. From Land's End to the Lizard, the Atlantic waves rolled across Mount's Bay on to the almost deserted shore. Inland, the towns of Marazion and Helston were joined by tracks. There was a single road to Penzance, but there was only one cart in the town as late as 1778; and pack horses were in use in all the country districts. This was a land where the smuggler was king, a man like Captain Harry Carter of Prussia Cove.

Harry Carter was one of a family of ten children. His father Francis had moved from Shropshire to Cornwall to rent a small farm and work in the mines. His mother Agnes brought up two daughters and eight sons, of whom John was the eldest. Harry and John were inseparable companions, and when all the boys played at soldiers one or the other would be King of Prussia — such was the fame of Frederick the Great at that time — and later when both were smugglers John's house on the clifftop was known as the King's house, and the small harbour below became Prussia Cove.

The Cove lay to the east of the sharp headland of Cudden Point. It was really two coves divided by a small island, the Enys, the western side being Bessey's Cove, but it was so secluded from the land side and the sea that it was impossible to see what boats lay in harbour until one came right to the cliff edge. The Carters made a roadway down the cliff to cross the rocks below the high-water mark. They made tracks into the caves near the water's edge which they connected by tunnels through the hillside to the house above. They cleared an anchorage to make a well concealed position which they could defend with cannon when necessary. Only Praa Sands and the Looe Bar broke the rock infested coastline between them and the Lizard.

This we know from Harry Carter's autobiography. He had no formal schooling but he could read 'in the Great Book' when he was nine, before going 'to work to stamps' — in the tin mine — until he was 16. Then he joined his elder brothers and the 'Cove Boys', going fishing and smuggling with them, and 'sometimes with Folston (Folkestone) people and sometimes with Irish'. They were wreckers as well. When a Dutch ship loaded with claret was wrecked off Helston in 1750 it was cleared of cargo and spars within 24 hours, and anyone resisting the robbers was killed, while the Customs men dared not interfere.

32

Why did Harry Carter confess, admittedly late in life, to such crimes? His autobiography was an authentic account of a notorious smuggler at a time when the Cornish trade was at its peak. It confirmed his reputation as a popular hero and a good humoured man in a community where he was well known. It is clear that the Carters controlled the smuggling around Mount's Bay. Harry and John were the leaders, but the whole family was involved, and as a group they were superior to the rough and reckless men who made up their crews. A local tale was that the Carter brothers once broke open the Customs warehouse in Penzance and took back confiscated goods which they had brought into the town, explaining that honest smugglers did not break bargains with their customers. That they were supported by farmers, merchants and even local magistrates is certain. They had contacts in London and at the Admiralty as well. Gentlemen liked to have their snuff and spirits duty free; ladies valued their perfume, fine lace and tea. Tax on these goods landed openly at a British port made them enormously expensive, so everyone of quality

secretly welcomed the successful smuggler and laughed at the Customs officer and the Exciseman whom he outwitted.

But Captain Carter wrote his life story for other reasons. He was a Methodist. He wrote as an act of penance for a misspent life, asking the Lord to make his book 'a blessing to every soul that read it, for Christ's sake, amen'. When he was nine years old he had been powerfully affected by the conversion of his elder brother Francis to Wesleyanism, and he was himself much troubled by visions in his lifetime. At the same time, he tells us, he could never resist the temptation of wealth and excitement, and he often came devoutly out of a religious meeting only to meet his old companions within a 100 yards and fall in with a scheme for a night run to Roscoff or Guernsey bringing brandy and tobacco.

At 19 Harry had learnt to write to keep his own accounts. At 23 he was running a small sloop with a two man crew and smuggling 'with very great success' from St Malo to Prussia Cove. He made enough profit to have a new 18-ton sloop built, and bought an old cutter into which he put a ten man crew. 'I began to think something of myself at this time,' he writes, 'and wanted to be noted as a good sort of man.' He would not allow swearing on board. The Carters were

24 Botallack, a Cornish tin mine. Miners were said to be violent characters; it is hardly surprising that against such men and such coastlines the revenue officers stood little chance.

running several vessels 'and being a speculating family was not satisfied with small things'. A week's good running might bring a profit of £1000. At the beginning of the American War they built a new cutter of 60 tons, 'expecting to make our fortunes in a hurry', because it was one of the first of its type in England and could easily outsail the Revenue boats. Harry approached certain gentlemen in London to obtain an Admiralty Commission to sail and fight as a privateer under the British flag. Then he could combine piracy with smuggling, get rich quick and be a fine fellow and patriot as well.

He was not so lucky. At Christmas 1777 he was sailing light to Guernsey for a cargo when he sprang the bowsprit and had to put into St Malo for repairs. The cutter was boarded by the French and put under armed guard; its captain was arrested and thrown into jail accused of piracy — 'their pretence nevertheless not being altogether unreasonable,' he admits, 'I having 16 carriage guns on board and 36 men without any papers.' As the cell door slammed shut on him for the first time in his life he wept bitterly: 'the cutter which was my god had gone. All the ten thousand pounds I expected to get privateering was gone.' A few hours later when 18 members of his crew had joined him in the cell he was leading them in a song, and a few weeks later, when they had all become prisoners of war instead of pirates with the outbreak of war between England and France, they were transferred inland to Josselin and placed on parole.

John Carter had meanwhile come over to St Malo to seek the release of the cutter and his brother, but he too was arrested, and it was not until November 1779 that the Lords of the Admiralty in London arranged their release in exchange for two French gentlemen. The Carter brothers got back home to find the family fortunes in a low state, but by the New Year they were at sea again running on credit offered by Guernsey merchants who valued their trade with England as much as the smugglers themselves.

From what Harry Carter tells us the normal practice of the smuggler was to lie offshore while the captain and a few men rowed in to the beach to make contact with others waiting for them. When the coast was clear a signal would be made to the ship to come inshore and discharge its cargo into small boats which would ferry the goods ashore. Even on a calm night it was skilled and dangerous work. Once off the Welsh coast Carter was surprised by a naval patrol boat while he was acting as contact man on the beach. His crew cut and ran for it, that is they cut their anchor cable, hoisted sail and got away, but their captain was caught and imprisoned for twelve weeks before friends at the Admiralty effected his release.

Risks of this sort were part of his life. His vessel might be seized as a pirate, com-

25 Cornish wreckers. Their activities were denounced by Wesley.

mandeered by the Royal Navy as a temporary warship and ordered to serve the Crown; he and his crew might be 'pressed' by the Press Gang or arrested as smugglers. At all times he had to risk being attacked at sea. After the American War he put out two vessels, an armed cutter and a new lugger mounting 20 guns, which worked together and could defend themselves. He was doing good business between Guernsey and Prussia Cove. After one trip his vessels were lying at anchor in Newlyn roads when an express messenger from the Customs Office at St Ives ordered him to sea to search for a Dunkirk privateer called the *Black Prince* operating in the Bristol Channel. Not wishing to anger the officials, and no doubt on the principle of live and let live, Carter put to sea and after a three day search found the enemy off Padstow. In a fight lasting several hours he drove the pirate ship down Channel, but the lugger

was holed and as the weather worsened was lost with 14 men. Carter picked up the rest and reached the Mumbles safely. 'In this action,' he wrote, 'I made the greatest outward show of bravery and exposed myself to the greatest dangers, but was always struck with horror of the mind as not being fit to die.' He reassured himself with the knowledge that even Anson said that he was frightened before going into action.

Within the year the hunter had become the hunted again. Smuggling off Cawsand, near Falmouth, he was surprised by two boats from a patrolling man-of-war and boarded. The jack tars quickly overpowered his crew, and Carter was knocked unconscious by a blow from a broadsword and left for dead on the deck. One of the naval boats slipped its towline and began to drift away, and as the sailors manned the other boat to go and make it fast Carter came to his senses. He crept along the deck and threw himself over the side. After a while he swam ashore and hid behind the rocks

26 **The press-gang at work.**

until the Navy had given up the search.

When some of his confederates, including his brother Charles, came looking for survivors they found him too badly injured to cry for help. He had been recognized in the fight and was a wanted man with a price of £300 on his head. They got him back to Marazion and for weeks moved him by night from one house to another to avoid capture. A doctor who was brought to treat his wounds was met by a member of the gang at some distance from where Carter was hiding and was brought to the house blindfolded. Later he was taken back blindfold to the same place.

By the autumn of 1788 Harry was well enough to spend his nights down on the beach with the Cove Boys, 'drinking grog until the grey of the morning', when he went back into hiding and worked on improving his knowledge of navigation. He tells us that his wife Elizabeth, whom he married in 1786, visited him secretly but he had decided to quit the country for a time and in October 1788 he said goodbye to his wife and daughter Betsy. His brother John rowed him out into Mount's Bay to meet a ship bound for Leghorn. In Italy the ship's captain got a freight for Barcelona, and then loaded brandy for New York. This was welcome news to Carter. In New York there was a Methodist Society, and he had now been stricken with conscience for his misdeeds. As he crossed the Atlantic he wished that he could be tied to a rope and thrown over the stern of the ship to atone for his sins. In New York he assumed the name of Captain Harry and later joined the Methodists in Baltimore, working for a time as a fieldhand with negroes from sunrise to sunset: 'I never was so happy in all my life as I was at that time.'

In July 1790 the chance came to return to England. He met a captain he had once known from the West Indies, looking for a navigator to take his vessel back to England. Carter had his charts and quadrant with him, and quickly struck a bargain by which in return for charting a course home he would be landed in Mount's Bay. As Land's End came into sight the captain took Carter forward and confessed that he himself was a pirate on the run, since he had stolen a loaded cargo vessel in England which he had sailed to New York and sold to buy his present sloop. He did not know the Channel, and begged Carter to stay and navigate to Calais, which the latter did in exchange for more promises of wealth and freedom later. In the Channel they met a fleet of West Indiamen with a naval escort, their boats out pressing men for service from passing ships. Carter nailed American colours to the mast and sailed on through them, ready to take his chance in a fight. Off Calais they found a pilot for Dunkirk and arrived there in September 1790.

Going up the harbour he saw the brig Betsy from Truro, bound for Falmouth from St Petersburg with a cargo of hemp

27 **Smugglers hiding their crates and kegs. The entrance to the caves used by the Carter family was hidden at high tide.**

and iron. In a few minutes a bond was made, and Harry Carter was back in the house of his brother Charles at Keneggy before Christmas, greeted as one returned from the dead. He had so changed that the Cove Boys did not recognize him until he spoke to them. He thanked God for his deliverance. On the following Sunday he went to preach at Trevean Church, 'where I had a blessed time; I was a wonder to myself. Every power of my soul was fully engaged in the work. I found great freedom to speak with the people in my simple way.'

By February 1791 he had made himself so conspicuous by his preaching that questions were being asked. How was a wanted man able to move about so openly without fear of arrest? He decided to go abroad again, but his brothers persuaded him to think of the family business, and so he sailed from Prussia Cove in an open boat for Roscoff, where he operated as a land agent for his brother John. He soon had a house at Roscoff and another inland at Morlaix, where he made a reputation for himself as a discreet man of business and a man of God, being asked to preach to the English community in the town: 'about 20 or 30 took off their hats and sat down — I began to tremble and sweat and could scarcely hold a hymn book in both hands. I gave out a verse and began to sing and, praise be to God, before I had sung the second verse I found life coming, and an uncommon degree of liberty, and the people all listened with the greatest attention.'

The smuggling prospered and Harry was able to go home at Christmas 1792 for a family reunion, but he was back on French soil by the time war broke out between England and France in 1793. With other British subjects he was arrested and placed on parole. 'I was not in the least afraid of all the lions in France,' he writes, but once the Terror started he was in prison under armed guard, with rumours flying everywhere that the British were to be placed on an uninhabited island off Brest and left to starve to death. French 'aristos' awaiting the guillotine were often brought to the prison at Landernau, but in December 1793 Carter and his friends — for so they had become by this time — were moved to Morlaix. Under the Law of Suspects they could be sentenced to death at any time. Food was short and Carter records that for the first time since 1789 he had to drink water: 'I had not one farthing of money. Every moment of time was far more precious than fine gold.' He had taken to long periods of fasting and self-examination in preparation to meet his Maker. The prisons were so full that in July 1794 he was transferred to the Convent of the Carmelites, taken over as a prison, but unknown to him Robespierre had been executed and the Reign of Terror was at an end. He was moved back to Morlaix and eventually freed in January 1795.

In June he was back in Roscoff, 'to see my old friends there, where I was received like a king.' He met Mr and Mrs McCulloch, whom he had come to know and respect in prison. They secured passports and in August 1795 he took passage for Falmouth in a Danish frigate, where he saw his wife and daughter Betsy, now nearly nine years old. A few days later and he was reunited with his brothers John, Charles and Francis, going in thanksgiving to pray at meetings in Breague, Churchtown and Rinsey, and finding that his old misdemeanours had been officially forgotten.

For the rest of his life he lived quietly with his family farming a small estate and adding to his reputation as a Methodist preacher and man of God. He maintained a discreet silence about his brothers, who were still active with the Cove Boys for some years yet, but along the coast and in the little hamlets of Germoe, St Hilary, Perranuthnoe and the hinterland, Captain Harry Carter had become a legend in his own lifetime.

5 THE FILE MAKER:
Peter Stubs

The bounty of nature on Sheffield town smiles,
Yet could other trades work if we did not make files?

This couplet was written by Alexander Stephens of Sheffield about two hundred years ago. It shows the importance of the ordinary steel file, such as we might buy today in any ironmongers, in the manufacturing work of earlier generations of men and women. Even today every workman who has to provide his own set of tools

28   **The tools of the trade: in the centre is an anvil with a file blank resting on a swage. The wedge-shaped chisels were struck with a variety of weighted hammers.**

for the job still carries a file. In the eighteenth century there were no powered lathes and emery wheels; power then came from wind or water mills and from the strength of animals and the human frame. The workers of those days needed tools which they could use by hand, and everyone who worked with metal, wood, stone, leather or textiles needed a file. Files had to be made of the hardest steel and that steel usually came from Sheffield.

The files made by Peter Stubs of Warrington were said to be the best in England. The trade mark *PS* stamped on the heel or handle end of his files was recognized throughout Europe and North America. In a manner resembling modern advertizing the men working for Brindley and the Duke of Bridgewater said that they preferred the *PS* files to all others. 'As we are building barracks for soldiers all of wood,' wrote Thomas Kirkup of Sunderland, during the French wars, more urgently than eloquently, 'the *PS* files must be supplied.' Every millwright and joiner in the expanding textile industry needed a file to ease the running of the spindles; every shipwright and sawyer in the ports needed files for shaping wood and sharpening saws.

Peter Stubs bought his steel from Sheffield. He always kept in close touch with Sheffield steel merchants and learned much from them as he made his way in the trade. He was a self-made man. His father and grandfather had been curriers or leather dressers, but when we first hear of Stubs he was already a file maker, aged 21, married to Mary Sutton. Ten years later he was landlord of the *White Bear* in Bridge Street, Warrington, and was combining file making with brewing and innkeeping. By 1802 he had set up substantial workshops and warehouses in what is now Scotland Road.

The files on which his fortune rested were all made by hand. At some time in his career he made files of every type and size, but his speciality was the small high grade steel file required by clockmakers, machine makers, whitesmiths and cotton spinners. He made files for goldsmiths in London, comb makers in Chester, pin makers in Bury, hook makers in Kendal, shoemakers in Manchester and gunsmiths in Wednesbury. For dentists all over the country he made tiny files 'for taking the decayed part out of teeth by twisting them round'. Large employers of labour like the Carron Ironworks and the New Lanark Mills ordered his files by the hundred dozen at a time, and as his business grew he was astute enough to find out what products made by his customers were selling well. With this guide he expanded his activities into comb making, glassware, school slate and slate pencil making and was part owner of vessels taking his goods to the Baltic.

He made his way in the trade by hard work and good business contacts, but it was not easy. Early in their married life his wife had earned extra money by letting a room and taking in washing. During her many pregnancies — she had 18 children — she had gone out as a wet nurse to persons of quality and had managed the inn. Their grandmother Mrs Johnson had lived with them to help with the children, and a brother-in-law Thomas Sutton had worked in the yard and had been the cobbler for the whole family. As the Stubs family rose in the world Mrs Stubs could afford a hairdresser, had a maidservant and a pony-gig; their children had a nurse and were taught by a schoolmaster for a fee of 18 guineas a year. By the turn of the century Peter Stubs was less like the 'little maister' of 1777 than the new nineteenth-century factory owner, but he never quite achieved this status because he could not persuade enough of his workers to accept factory conditions of work, with a regular routine and regular rates of pay. These had to wait until John Stubs took over the firm after his father's death in 1806.

In the third quarter of the eighteenth century South Lancashire had become a centre for small metal trades. By the 1770s there was a growing port at Liverpool and a developing commercial centre at Manchester. Warrington was well sited on the coalfield, with a navigable river linked to a canal system. Stage coaches from London to Liverpool passed through the town twice each weekday, and on every other day there were coaches going regularly to Manchester, Wigan and York, with connections to all the industrial centres of England. They carried light parcel luggage, and Stubs used them for urgent orders, but his usual method of supply was by waggon. Steel brought in this way from Sheffield to Manchester took two and a half days coming via Hathersage and Chapel-en-le-Frith. From Manchester to Warrington the steel might come by canal at the cheap rate of three-pence per hundredweight. Despite this Stubs preferred to send most things by waggon with carriers whom he knew personally. There were occasions when waggon loads of steel might be stuck on Blackstone Edge in three feet of snow, but he still thought them more reliable than barge transport.

When Stubs started making files he made them from start to finish, and by agreement sold them through the steelmakers or wholesalers who had supplied the steel. To begin with he had a small workshop and one apprentice, Benjamin Jolley, who went out to deliver small orders by hand. In the early days of the business most customers paid in cash, but a Liverpool firm of tool makers once gave Stubs enough material to make a new suit instead. He was trying to build up his trade reputation and professional standing at this time, and as well as being well dressed wanted to develop a fine copperplate style of handwriting for his business letters. He used to practise writing sentences on the back of old bills: 'My kingdom for an horse said King Richard'

seems to have been his favourite example.

His workers were domestic out-workers, that is to say they did the work in their own homes. Sometimes they collected the work from Stubs and sometimes he sent it to them by waggon. There was usually an agreed date by which the work had to be finished and ready for collection. It was not unusual to find two generations in a family team, like the Appletons of Huyton, six of whom worked for him over a period of 30 years. His books, for example, show him on one occasion supplying them with cast steel and two large files called pottance files, which were used to scrape the 18 dozen small files which they undertook to make to order. He had initially set them up in the work by providing them with an anvil, bellows, an oilstone, vice and workbenches.

How was a file made at that time? Rods of steel cut into short lengths were heated before being placed on the anvil between two file moulds. The moulds were called swages. The forger struck the upper swage with a hammer until the hot steel assumed the moulded shape of the file, and then cleaned and cooled it while its surface was still soft enough to take the cutting chisel. Cutting the required pattern of ridges on the blank file with a hammer and chisel was a most important part of the work. Striking the chisel with a six pound hammer the file cutter made the first cut in the file and drew back the chisel a fraction of an inch before sliding it forward to feel the ridge made by the cut, then he struck again. An experienced man could do this so rapidly and skilfully that he made hundreds of cuts faster than the eye could follow, and the patterned surface of the newly made file emerged as if by magic beneath the chisel's edge.

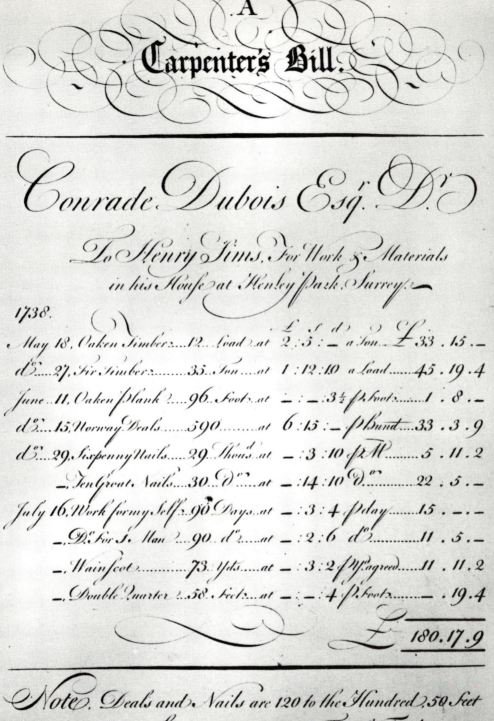

A
Carpenter's Bill.

Conrade Dubois Esq.r Dr

To Henry Sims, For Work & Materials
in his House at Henley Park, Surrey.

1738.

			£ s d	£
May 18, Oaken Timber	12	Load at	2 : 5 : — a Ton	33 . 15 . —
d.o 27, Fir Timber	35	Ton at	1 : 12 : 10 a Load	45 . 19 . 4
June 11, Oaken Plank	96	Foot at	— : — : 3½ p.foot	1 . 8 . —
d.o 15, Norway Deals	590	at	6 : 15 : — p.hund	33 . 3 . 9
d.o 29, Sixpenny Nails	29	Thous.d at	— : 3 : 10 p.M	5 . 11 . 2
—, Ten Groat Nails	30	D.o at	— : 14 : 10 D.o	22 . 5 . —
July 16, Work for my Self	90	Days at	— : 3 : 4 p.day	15 . — . —
—, D.o For 1 Man	90	d.o at	— : 2 : 6 d.o	11 . 5 . —
—, Wainscot	73	Yds at	— : 3 : 2 p.Y.d agreed	11 . 11 . 2
—, Double Quarter	58	Feet at	— : — : 4 p.foot	— . 19 . 4
			£	180.17.9

Note. Deals and Nails are 120 to the Hundred, 50 Feet
are a Load, and 40 Feet a Ton of Timber.

N: Dove scr.

It was hard, noisy and tiring work, recognized by the versifier Joseph Mather in 'The File Hewer's Lamentation':

Of slaving I am weary,
From June to January!
To nature it's contrary —
This I presume is fact.

Although without a stammer
Our Nell exclaims I clam her, [prevent
    from speaking]
I wield my six pound hammer
Till I am grown round-backed.

The tools were sent back to Stubs for hardening. A file was rubbed with charcoal to clean the bits of steel and pewter from its teeth and coated with a paste made from the dregs of beer barrels and malt dust. Carbon from this mixture entered the teeth of the file and gave it greater durability and strength. Here Stubs had the advice of his Sheffield friends, who were familiar with the new Huntsman process for making crucible steel. Files were heated and thrust into a solution of salt and water. The degree of heat, the amount of salt and the duration of immersion differed with different types

30 Tempering steel files after cutting.

of file and were suitably guarded secrets of the hardeners which were valued by customers. 'I will thank you to give the old hardener one shilling to drink', wrote one, 'desire him to temper them well.'

The files were finally cleaned and tested, before being oiled and wrapped in stout paper and packed in wooden boxes to await the carrier. Most carriers had covered waggons and operated over their own small but well known region. Three firms might be involved to get files, for example, from Warrington to Skipton, but Stubs always tried to persuade his carriers to attempt the whole journey to avoid loss or damage to goods in transit. He sometimes used Pickfords, both their waggons and their flyboat service. He sent his beer out by waggon as well.

There was usually a cash settlement between Stubs and his out-workers every two or three months. Since deductions had to be made for raw materials supplied it was not uncommon to find rough and ready credit arrangements being made. Mrs William Taylor normally took files made by her husband to Stubs at the *White Bear* and often received a cheese and a cask of beer in part payment. This was certainly not a modern industrial system at work but it suited the circumstances of the time. England was still a rural nation and most of its inhabitants made part of their living from the land. The file makers in their country cottages could farm a smallholding, keep a pig and work indoors when they pleased. The old songs and rhymes tell us that there was no work done on Saints' Days, which were Holy Days, and that the cottage workers honoured St Monday, St Tuesday and often St Wednesday as well. Then the whole family would set to work furiously in order to complete their agreed quota in time for the settlement day. If they did not deliver the goods in time they would risk losing an order for more work.

Why were the *PS* files, and indeed the

whole range of tools which Stubs was making by the turn of the century, so much better than others on the market? They were harder, cut better and lasted longer. Naturally Stubs would not reveal his trade secrets in such a competitive age, but it was said that his special recipe for mixing paste to cover the files during hardening made the vital difference. A popular explanation ascribed this to the quality of his beer at the *White Bear*, and the powerful residues in the bottom of the beer vats. Stubs did not take over the inn without appreciating the connection between brewing beer and chopping files, and he was not the only brewer and file cutter listed in the Liverpool Trades Directory.

He had taken the inn because he intended to make it the centre of his activities. Not merely was an inn a place where business could be transacted in comfort, but it could also be a direct selling point. Taverns and fairs were well known local exchanges for work orders and a supply of labour. Peter Stubs also saw that by taking over and extending the buildings around the coach-yard he might develop a manufactory. He could use different buildings for different stages of the work, with warehouses for storage of materials and finished goods. He could try to persuade his workpeople to come together, and he might put individuals on to those parts of the work which they could do best — that is to say he could specialize.

He was not the only employer trying to do this at this time. In Sheffield the Goddard family had set up their Abbeydale works making scythes and other agricultural tools with the same idea in mind. A factory system was taking shape in Lancashire and Cheshire in the mills. When Stubs built his file works in 1802 he sited the smithy and forges on one side of a cobbled yard with the cutting rooms above them. On another side were the hardening and finishing shops and on a third side the warehouse.

Being within easy reach at the *White Bear* he could supervise the work and guarantee its quality. All these early industrial employers had the same problems with workers who would only slowly change their ways. Stubs was sometimes in such difficulty getting men for his works that he hired the Sheffield Town Crier to go out calling for file forgers and apprentices.

He seems to have been as successful an innkeeper as he was a file maker. It was not only brewing ale and beer which occupied his time there. He built up a considerable business in barley, hops, malt and yeast. The quality of his malt drew almost as much praise as the strength of his files. His October Ale and his Brown Ale were so palatable that other innkeepers bought from him rather than make their own. His later interest in the manufacture and engraving of glassware derived from his success as a liquor salesman. The close relationship which existed between his business and his home must be obvious.

He was a convivial host who shared the recreations of his clients at the *White Bear*. He was not the austere Nonconformist industrialist, but was a patriotic Anglican who enjoyed a drink, a game of cards and a wager. When he did not meet his suppliers at the inn he went with them to the race meetings at Doncaster, Manchester and Chester. His deliveries to important customers sometimes included a Warrington river salmon or a box of sprats. At Christmas time this would be a goose or a brace of hares. The merchants of Sheffield made social visits to the Stubs household and their children spent holidays in each other's homes. During the war with France Stubs established a 'Soldiers' Room' at the inn and was proud to provide a mount and a sword for his son John when the latter became a Volunteer in the 'Redbreasts', as the Warrington contingent was known. Another of his interests was in providing a 'Box' at the inn for the poor and needy,

31 **A brew-house in 1747: the top right-hand corner shows the exterior.**

from which donations might be made to war widows or workmen absent through injury or illness. He was known to buy medicines for their families. This reminds us that the eighteenth century inn was something more than a place of refreshment, and that it contributed to the social services of the time.

From about 1801 his sons began to take a more direct interest in the business. They went out as travellers, financial agents and supervisors in the works. From this we can conclude that the founder of the firm was in failing health. His letters show that he was suffering from some bronchial complaint, and although he took the fashionable water treatments at Spas like Buxton his condition gradually got worse. He died at Warrington in 1806, aged 49, and was buried in the Parish Churchyard. His career is a typical example of that first generation of industrialists and factory owners who transformed the working habits of the people of this country and introduced a new age.

6 THE GOVERNESS:
Ellen Weeton

'I would not be understood to argue that woman is superior to man; I should blush to advance so weak an opinion. I only affirm that they are *equal*, and ought to be treated as such in every respect.' However much this may remind us of Miss Bennett confounding Mr D'Arcy these are not the words of one of Jane Austen's fictitious heroines. Yet Ellen Weeton's story lacks the touch of true romance, for though she is equally worthy of our sympathy and admiration she has, by the time she tells it, neither youth, beauty nor riches.

She was born on Christmas Day 1776 and christened Nelly after the name of her father's ship. He had been hoping for a boy, so his wife Mary chose the name to endear the baby to her father. Thomas Weeton was the captain of a slaver, running from the Lune at Lancaster to West Africa and the West Indies. He worked for a Quaker family, the Rawlinsons, and his wife Mary was their distant kinswoman. Like other men of his day Tom Weeton's ambition was to earn £10,000 and set himself up in a position of independence, but his career had taken a more dangerous turn and he had been commandeered and given Letters of Marque to fight as a British privateer in the American war. Six years later, when his wife and family were awaiting his return, news came that he had been killed in action and buried in Jamaica. Suddenly Mary Weeton found herself practically destitute with two children, Ellen and baby Tom, and the compensation which she had expected from war prize money denied her.

Mrs Weeton was an intelligent woman with a relatively good background and education. She had been a ladies' maid to the titled Hoghton family and had spent some time in London, but now she had to take in lodgers to supplement the £30 or £40 a year which came from a small estate left by her husband at Sunderland Point, near Lancaster. She had savings of £500 but that was not enough to support a family, her ailing mother and orphan niece, so in 1784 the household moved to Up Holland, near Wigan, where the cost of living was cheaper and Mrs Weeton could be near her sister Mrs Margaret Barton. Four years later she rented and opened a village school there. 'My mother had no servant,' says Ellen, 'and her life as well as mine was from this time a life of slavery.'

All this we now know from Ellen Weeton's Journal, a collection of letters, essays and reminiscences which she compiled over many years, but which she never intended to be seen by anyone in her lifetime, and then even after her death only by one person: 'It is for my little Mary principally that I write this. My child will know no more of her mother than what she may learn from these pages.'

Her tragic tale might have remained untold had not a letter book been discovered by Edward Hall in 1925, while browsing in a second hand bookshop in Wigan. Mr Hall was an antiquarian book dealer from Surrey but a Lancashire man by birth; the find aroused his interest and by the detective work characteristic of his trade he traced other volumes and pieced together this picture of an eighteenth-century governess. At least this is how Ellen Weeton liked to think of herself, although she sometimes does not seem to be more than a companion or housekeeper: 'A *governess* is almost shut out of society; not choosing to associate with servants, and not being treated as an equal by the heads of the house or their visitors, she must possess some fortitude and strength of mind to render herself tranquil or happy.' There is both pride and poignancy in this self-appraisal by a lonely, ageing woman, intelligent enough to see her life wasting away but neither attractive nor sociable enough to prevent it. Her quick mind had a sharp tongue to match: 'It is my misfortune or my fault, I wish I could tell which, not to conciliate the regard of those I dwell with — at least some of them.' In other words she simply could not get on with people — her sense of superiority made her awkward and tongue-tied in company. So this plain, pimply woman, wearing the black or grey clothes which were most easily brushed clean or mended, locked herself in her room when work was done and wrote letter after letter to anyone she could — she called it her 'epistolatory conversation'.

At 12 Ellen was helping her mother 'to teach and do the work of the house, and in sewing for hire'. During the day she had pupils for company but seldom met adults. She wrote letters to her brother on her slate. Sometimes she went with her mother to a Methodist meeting in a shoemaker's house, where Mr Bannister, a clergyman, carefully avoided saying the regular prayers lest he incur the Bishop's censure. Ellen's life became lonelier when Tom was sent to Mr Braithwaite's Academy in Up Holland, then at 14 he went off to Preston to become

32   A typical picture of a village schoolmistress with her class.

33   The schoolhouse, the cottage and the garden of the Priory.

a solicitor's apprentice. Ellen stayed in the village. Her mother, 'thinking that I should be entirely ruined for any useful purpose in life', refused to allow her to study literature or languages: 'Oh! How I have burned to learn Latin, French, the Arts, the Sciences, anything rather than the dog-trot way of sewing, teaching, writing copies and washing dishes every day.'

In 1797 Mary Weeton died, worn out at 51. Ellen paid the funeral expenses of £49 — an enormous sum, but less than they had paid for her father — and carried on the school, where 14 scholars each paid six shillings a quarter. While she remained single Ellen had the interest on a £100 bond left to her by her mother, but all the estate rent had to go to Tom, plus whatever Ellen could save from her meagre earnings.

Existing in grinding poverty on a diet of bread and potatoes Ellen lived in hope of a rosy future when the brother whom she idolized would come back to the home she kept for him. For this she had already declined one offer of marriage. Tom Weeton completed his training in 1802 and went to London for a three month's holiday. He returned to Up Holland for a few weeks, amazed to discover that he would now have to share the Sunderland Point rent with his sister, then left to find a place of his own in Wigan, shortly meeting and marrying Jane Scott, the daughter of a factory owner there. He aimed to establish himself as an attorney, eventually becoming Clerk to the Magistrates in Leigh.

This slight which Ellen endured at her brother's hand became a commonplace experience later, yet she showered affection on him and was blind to his ingratitude and malevolence. She offered the newly-weds a home but they soon left her cottage, the new Mrs Weeton having her own decided opinions about the relative status of an impoverished, elder sister-in-law. Never friends, Ellen's sharp tongue and Jane's social ambitions meant that the two women would grow farther apart.

It seems to have been about 1805 that Miss Weeton first thought of becoming a governess, but the Scott family was against it because her 'degrading profession of schoolmistress' might become known to their detriment. Ellen tried unsuccessfully for a post at Crofton Academy with Miss Magnall, famous for her *Historical Questions and Answers*: 'I only thought of it as a means of fitting me for a governess in a private family, for where so many are taught, surely I might have learned something.'

She was by this time writing and copying her letters, priding herself on a beautifully legible quill script and taking up to five hours to complete her longest compositions. This lonely, spirited woman wrote for self-fulfilment and for posterity. 'I have become so much accustomed to quiet I cannot write without it,' she says, 'I copy all my letters. It is an amusement to me to read them over again — again to recall former ideas, and incidents long past.' For years she wrote principally to brother Tom, but the Braithwaites, mother and daughters, were more trustworthy, lifelong friends. Miss Chorley, the daughter of a retired Liverpool tanner, was an arrogant and acrimonious spinster who often made sport with Miss Weeton's letters among her circle — but Ellen was a tenacious correspondent whose insistence on prompt replies must have been trying. Tom called her letters 'much ado about nothing'. There was also the avaricious and unpleasant Aunt Barton, to whom Ellen must needs be civil. What are we to think of an elderly woman in more fortunate circumstances who could *lend* her 20-year-old orphan niece one penny to buy a bandage for a badly cut ankle, caused by the torn clog-iron of one of her pupils?

Miss Weeton wrote to any friends she made. She was not a selfish woman, but she was self-centred, and these people made up her world. Her letters do not mention

34 An example of Miss Weeton's careful and legible script: a letter to Miss Winckley.

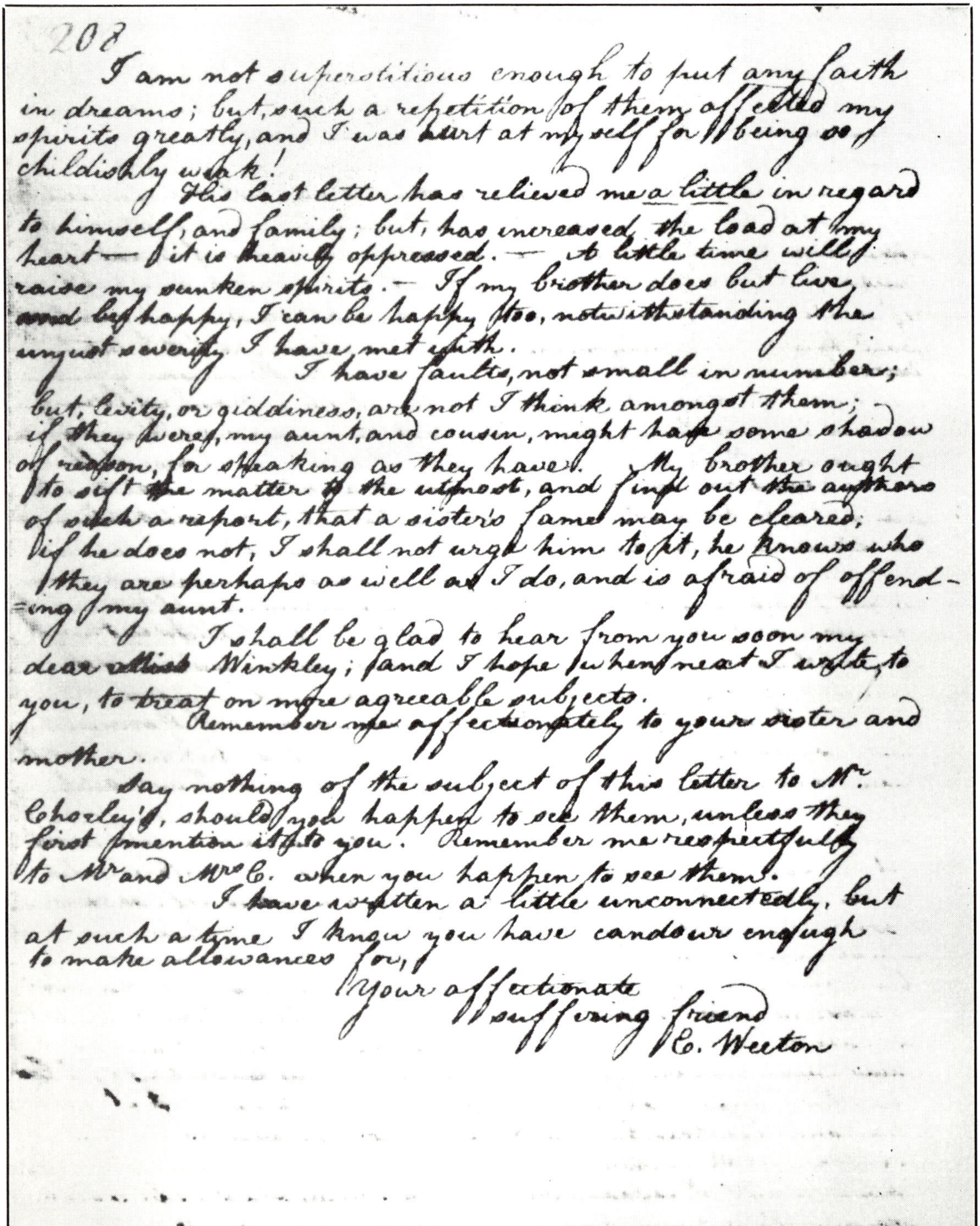

208

I am not superstitious enough to put any faith in dreams; but, such a repetition of them affected my spirits greatly, and I was hurt at myself for being so childishly weak!

His last letter has relieved me a little in regard to himself, and family; but, has increased the load at my heart — it is heavily oppressed. — A little time will raise my sunken spirits. — If my brother does but live, and be happy, I can be happy too, notwithstanding the unjust severity I have met with.

I have faults, not small in number; but, levity, or giddiness, are not I think amongst them; if they were, my aunt, and cousin, might have some shadow of reason, for speaking as they have. My brother ought to sift the matter to the utmost, and find out the authors of such a report, that a sister's fame may be cleared; if he does not, I shall not urge him to it, he knows who they are perhaps as well as I do, and is afraid of offending my aunt.

I shall be glad to hear from you soon my dear ~~Miss~~ Winkley; and I hope when next I write, to you, to treat on more agreeable subjects.

Remember me affectionately to your sister and mother.

Say nothing of the subject of this letter to Mr Chorley's, should you happen to see them, unless they first mention it to you. Remember me respectfully to Mr and Mrs C. when you happen to see them.

I have written a little unconnectedly, but at such a time I know you have candour enough to make allowances for,

Your affectionate
suffering friend
E. Weeton

famous names and events: once she described Miss Chorley as 'what Buonaparte is to Europe — a scourge'; in 1809 she wrote that her earnings were £60 a year 'Income Tax paid'; in Huddersfield she made reference to the Luddites, but these were exceptions. Always she wrote about her own ordinary activities and those of her correspondents.

In 1808, now 32 and called 'an old maid' by her brother, Ellen Weeton decided to make a change. She bought the tumble-down cottage adjoining her own, closed the school, sold her furniture and let the properties — leaving the home she had known for 24 years without regret — to become a paying guest with the Smith family at Beacon's Gutter, Kirkdale. Tom Weeton had offered her a home for 30 guineas a year; she found one for a fifth of that sum. For a time she was happy with Edwin and Betty Smith and their six-year-old son.

Mr Smith was a journeyman in a tobacco warehouse in Liverpool, but lived in this isolated farmhouse on the banks of the Mersey where his wife took in guests in summer who came for the fashionable salt water, sea-bathing cure. Enjoying the luxury of a fire in her upstairs room, Ellen sat at the window writing, watching the ships and the people on the shore. She helped with her needle and in the house and garden. Once she witnessed a ship-wreck, with the crew clearing the cargo so fast that two fields nearby were covered with Irish linen.

Occasionally she visited friends, like the Chorleys or the Winkleys in Liverpool. She once returned by canal boat from a visit to Aunt Barton. The journey took all day — with a cook in the stern serving bacon and eggs, beefsteak and mutton chops — too rich for Miss Weeton in both senses, while the quality sat in the bows with their picnic baskets. She envied Mrs Smith her married state and wrote to Tom that she was 'a second Mrs Weeton' in her reluctance

to get up in the morning, but she could not tolerate arguments between husband and wife which sometimes ended in blows, or with Betty locked out for the night.

Miss Weeton never enjoyed an income sufficient to give her real independence; nor did she have the personality and background to be accepted in that genteel society to which she aspired. She once wrote ruefully that with a knowledge of French she might have earned £100 a year, but this was always beyond her. Consequently she had to take positions which never quite came up to her expectations, like hundreds of thousands of other domestics, servants of one sort or another, who scraped and saved to be respectable 'in service'.

In October 1809 she moved her lodgings to the Winkleys, but was put out to find that she was not expected to join the company when callers were entertained. 'The more I see of society and the prouder I grow,' she wrote, 'perhaps it is because the class I have got amongst are rather below the middling station than above it. Should I ever be enabled to rise a little higher I may again become as humble in my own estimation as I used to be — but of rising in this world there is no prospect.'

In this frame of mind she jumped at the chance of becoming 'a Governess to super-intend the Education of a Young Lady in the neighbourhood of Kendal.' Miss Winkley had shown her the advertisement; Ellen asked for 30 guineas a year and got the post — 'a transition from an obscure street in Liverpool to an elevated situation near the head of Windermere Lake — enough to turn my brain a little.' Her employer was Mr Pedder, a widower of 34, and a member of a well known Preston banking family. His ten-year-old daughter suffered from fits, but she was not to be Miss Weeton's principal charge. Ellen was to be companion to the second Mrs Pedder, a pretty 17-year-old dairymaid, with whom Pedder had eloped to marry over the anvil at Gretna Green, but who lacked the education to fit into polite society. Their household was at Dove's Nest, near Ambleside.

At last Miss Weeton seemed to have achieved her ambition. Her income was twice what it had been at Up Holland and she was 'treated with a degree of deference and respect'. During the next two years she became friendly with the Lakeland painter, William Green and his family, and later stayed with them. She soon knew Hawkshead and Grasmere well; she rowed on Windermere, attended the regatta and watched the Lakeland games. Two notable days were when she climbed Fairfield and the Langdales, with the Pedders and others in a cheerful company.

But the picture had its darker side: 'Wherever I go,' she wrote, 'I must expect some unpleasant circumstances.' Several of her correspondents had stopped writing after the circulation of a story that she had 'gone off with a gentleman'. This scandalmongering was the work of Tom

35 Miss Weeton's employer at High Royd, Joseph Armitage: 'Mr A. is engaged in the woollen trade, has a handsome fortune of his own.'

Weeton and his cousin Miss Latham, both of whom hoped to exclude Ellen from the will of the ailing Aunt Barton, so that some few pounds might come instead to them. Tragedy was added to this slander when the young Miss Pedder was burned to death when her apron caught fire. Mrs Pedder gave up books for cards and her husband turned to drink, becoming abusive to the female members of the household. This could not be endured, and Miss Weeton left her employer and returned to Liverpool.

Before taking another post she spent a month on holiday in the Isle of Man, and her journal tells of some remarkable exploits, such as climbing Snaefell on her own to see 'three kingdoms and a principality'. She thought Manx women pitiable, with their bare and bleeding feet, but what must they have thought of this grey-haired bony woman, with her 'small slouch straw hat, grey stuff jacket and petticoat, a white net bag in one hand and a parasol in the other' as she strode out alone over mountain roads and tracks in walks which sometimes covered 35 miles?

Then she was back to two more years of domestic servitude, this time with the Armitage family of High Royd, Huddersfield, in the woollen trade, with a young family growing more numerous every year. Yorkshire folk she found 'a plodding, money-getting good sort of people'. High Royd was on the moor; there were more donkeys than people and Ellen's life was a busy one of 'uncertain and perpetual activity'. Her complaint was the same — Mrs Armitage did not treat her as one of the family — and when she left she said that she had been 'a tenfold closer prisoner than any other governess in the neighbourhood'.

This was in July 1814. Within two months Ellen Weeton's life had changed unbelievably for the worse. She had married 'a monster of a husband' to whom she had, by law, surrendered all her worldly possessions and was henceforth to be kept penniless. Tom

Weeton and his wife had spread the lie that she had been pregnant before the marriage. The only explanation of this amazing change must be the blindness, loneliness and near desperation of Ellen Weeton herself — clutching at the illusion of love and security, and forgetful of the knowledge of her brother's past deceit. She had not heard from Tom for three years. In July when she was staying at Up Holland with the Braithwaites Tom Weeton called on her, supposedly to repay a debt. At the same time he must have commended to his sister the name and character of Aaron Stock.

Stock was a widower with two grown-up daughters. He had a cotton factory in Chapel Lane, Wigan, in premises which he leased from Tom Weeton's mother-in-law. His business was in a shaky state and he needed what extra capital he could get. Tom Weeton stood to gain the £100 bond under his mother's will if Ellen Weeton ever married. A few words of flattery and address and the 'job' was done — for so it clearly seems — with our elderly heroine writing to her brother, 'on the day you receive this, I shall most probably have resigned my prospects of future happiness or misery for this life, into the hands of another'.

Once Stock had got his hands on her money he set about driving her out of her mind and out of his life. Ellen Weeton's letters stopped abruptly and it is only when she began to write again years later that we can piece together the story of what happened. Her daughter Mary was born in June, 1815. Already she realized how she had been deceived. Her grown-up step-daughters insulted her; her husband kept a mistress. Deprived entirely of money, physically beaten and periodically locked up, turned into the street and deliberately starved of food, Ellen Weeton had reached the lowest point in her life.

In November, 1816, she writes: 'My husband is my terror, my misery! and I have little doubt, will be my death. I shall never live to educate Mary, unless I quit this place.' Imprisoned, threatened with the lunatic asylum, ridiculed, the poor woman escaped to Up Holland when she could, sometimes taking Mary with her, until in 1822 she was able to secure a deed of separation from Stock while losing custody of her daughter. Mary was sent to a boarding school at Parr Hall, St Helen's, a deplorable insitution run by Mr and Mrs Grundy, where Ellen was allowed to see her three times a year. Stock had agreed to allow her £70 a year, paid quarterly in arrears, more than a discredited wife might have expected in the circumstances but less, of course, than her investments might have been earning had she stayed single. During these unhappy seven years Aunt Barton and her husband had died, but money left to Ellen had gone by law to her husband.

Ellen crept back to Up Holland, to a 'poky parlour' at Ball's Farm, to stave off madness by commencing another letter book to a depleted circle of correspondents. She wrote now to Mary, but Aaron Stock made arrangements to intercept and destroy what letters he could. He blackened her character and Tom Weeton supported him, so that Ellen was branded as a deranged and untrustworthy person. There are sad stories of her attempts to meet Mary, walking over to Parr Hall each Sunday and attempting to tag along with the crocodile of school-children going to and from church, and in her search for respectability as a member of Hope Chapel, Wigan, under the protection of the Rev. William Marshall, who believed and helped her.

Not until 1824 does she seem to have recovered her health and spirits. Then we hear of her travelling to London as a companion to two young people, Miss Stopford and Master Barlow, who were visiting friends. Ellen rode cheaply and precariously on top of the coach. She had a two months' holiday, tramping about from morning till night without any fear, watching the new craze of ballooning, visiting the sights and sailing on the river: 'went for the first time to the British Museum and stayed nearly seven hours. My poor feet were sadly swelled, yet I could have no mercy on them, nor on my dinnerless stomach.'

Then it was back to Liverpool, again on the top seats, via Oxford and Birmingham. She had now moved to Mr and Mrs Tyrer's house at Prescot to be nearer to Mary and was building up a new circle of correspondents. Mrs Braithwaite and Miss Chorley were dead: Aunt Barton lay near Ellen's mother in Up Holland churchyard, as did Ellen's father-in-law Mr Stock. Ellen's letter books were, however, also coming to an end. She had suffered greatly from inflammation of the eyes since her marriage, but before giving up copying she recorded a Welsh holiday in 1825 during which she climbed Snowdon and walked miles among folk whose language she could not understand.

We know from records of Hope Chapel that she and her daughter were admitted to full membership there, and that they resided in Wigan again when Aaron Stock moved to Ashton-in-Makerfield to become part-owner of a coal mine, so it would seem that mother and daughter were happily re-united and welcomed back into a Christian community. There is a solitary letter to Tom

Weeton in 1837, who by this time had been retired in disgrace after the forgery of a will belonging to one of his clients, but there was no real contact between them despite her willingness to forget the past. He was busy tracing his ancestry, to establish for his wife's satisfaction that the Weetons were of noble birth, and Ellen offered what she knew of their history. Ellen Weeton herself disappears from our view in 1844, with her death listed in the Chapel records, and the Up Holland cottages passing to brother Tom at last. Lying in some unknown grave, as one of the millions of the insignificant poor, we can take leave of her in the words of one of her last letters:

The solitary life I lead is not from choice; I see no way of avoiding it. I am naturally of a lively, social turn, and to be often in the company of such as possess highly cultivated minds, would be a gratification to me, superior even to books. But God has said 'Set your affection on things above, and not on things on the earth.' — and therefore appears to have specially deprived me of all those things on which I could have set my affections. Thy will be done! I see Thy mercies and Thy Graciousness in this, and am thankful.

36 **This sketch of Standishgate, Wigan, in 1836 shows Ellen Weeton's residence on the extreme right.**

7 THE RIDING PREACHER:

Adam Clarke

Death was a constant companion in the life of eighteenth-century England. Sudden illness or injury often proved fatal. Infectious epidemics cut down rich and poor alike. With human life so cheap it was not surprising that those who were poorest and most degraded grasped with relief at the promise of heavenly life offered by a new religion. When Charles and John Wesley started a society at Oxford, whose members tried to lead a methodical life of prayer and good works — for which they were nicknamed 'Methodists' — they did not realize that they were starting a popular break-away culture in the Church which would influence the lives of thousands of ordinary folk from that time onwards. One of Wesley's helpers in spreading this faith was Adam Clarke.

He was not an ordained minister of religion but was what we would call a lay preacher. At that time he was described as a 'riding preacher', or a 'field preacher', because he rode on horseback from place to place, speaking four or five times in a day to large audiences, and preaching in the fields when he was not allowed to hold a meeting in church. Wherever he went he took the simple message of the Gospel. Near the end of his life he wrote: 'I have lived more than three score years and ten; I have read much, thought much and reasoned much, and the result is — I am persuaded of the simple unadulterated truth of no

book but the Bible. For nearly 50 years I have lived only for the support and credit of Methodism.'

Men like Clarke did their work because of the marvellous inspiration and organization of their leader John Wesley. He mapped out his life and theirs, and took religion directly into the lives of the people by preaching the Bible, because he was convinced that this was the only means of helping them. He told them that religion was an intensely personal emotion, and that if they really

37 **Adam Clarke, aged 33: 'Ye have not chosen me but I have chosen you.'**

believed in the redeeming power of Jesus Christ they would feel a spiritual change or 'conversion' which would give them an assurance of life after death. 'Guide Me O Thou Great Redeemer' was a hymn which exactly expressed Methodist teaching. Its popularity was greatest among the less educated; it gave hope and a purpose in life to those who felt lost, friendless and despairing. Methodists looked up to Heaven and forgot their earthly grievances. On the one hand it was a popular tranquillizer, but on the other hand it was revivalism — 'hell-fire preaching' — which was said by its critics to drive thousands of people into a state of religious emotion and hysteria.

Adam Clarke had experienced such a conversion while still a boy, working in the fields of Ireland. His father was a village schoolmaster near Londonderry. His mother, a keen Bible reader, had been converted to Methodism on the first visit of the preachers to Coleraine. John Brettell and Thomas Barber came to set up Classes and form Societies. The Methodist Class was a small, local group of about a dozen people. A number of Classes would form a Society, which was the largest of the local units. Each Class met weekly for prayer and paid a penny for a ticket of membership. The Society collected the money to build Methodist chapels. Classes and Societies were grouped together in regional Circuits,

which were visited by the preachers appointed to them. Every year there was a Conference presided over by John Wesley which all the preachers attended. 'Establish Class meetings and form Societies wherever you preach,' said Wesley, 'and you shall have attentive hearers.' This was his highly centralized organization which he controlled so completely that his enemies called him Pope John.

Adam Clarke and his brother went to school on alternate days because their father had rented a farm to help out his earnings as a schoolmaster. In summer they rose at four in the morning and worked a 12 hour day. In the evening the boy who had been to school taught his brother who had been left to work on the farm. Adam was fond of reading and got second hand books from wandering gipsies; he was a strong boy who could swim and ride well. He survived his father's teaching, and tells us that as soon as he could read he was given a copy of Lily's Latin Grammar with the advice: 'Go, Sir, and take up your Grammar. If you do not speedily get that lesson, I shall pull your ears as long as Jowler's (the family dog) and you shall be a beggar till the day of your death!'

At 18 he went to the Methodist Love-feast in Coleraine — the quarterly meeting —

38 **The first Methodist Conference, 25 June 1744.**

and afterwards joined the Society, being asked to lead classes in scripture reading. Going to a village, he would enter the first open door that he saw, saying 'Peace be to this house.' Then he would read a verse, ask the people to pray with him and go on to the next cottage. He continued his own studies in the Classics, French and Mathematics although apprenticed to a linen draper in the town, but he was devoted to his religious work and in June 1782 he was

39 **The insignia of office of the President of the Methodist Conference: the Bible used by Wesley on his journeys and the official seal.**

invited by Mr Bredin, the Superintendent of the Circuit, to preach his first sermon at New Buildings, Derry. Two months later Mr Bredin was appointed to an English Circuit. He had written to Wesley about Adam Clarke and was told to bring the boy with him, so that he might enter a school for Methodist preachers at Kingswood, Bristol. The ship on which they sailed to Liverpool was boarded by the Press Gang in the Mersey, but Clarke and Bredin both escaped. In Bristol Adam Clarke met John and Charles Wesley, whom he thought 'the most favoured instruments which God had employed since the days of the 12 apostles'. He stayed for some months at Kingswood and was then appointed to Trowbridge in Wiltshire, with Societies extending into Somerset and Dorset.

It is difficult for us today to imagine the daily work of these riding Methodist preachers, forever in the saddle between one meeting place and the next, delivering their first sermon at five in the morning and then on to another assembly, riding in all weathers and accepting every risk of the highway, and at the end being expected to give an uplifting or consolatory counsel. They always preached from a starting point in the Bible. Clarke said it was the only book he ever needed. But almost all of them used the circumstances and topics of the time to explain and enlarge their message. They told homely tales which their listeners could understand. They told of their own experiences. They interpreted the Parables.

Each one of them had a style of his own. When Clarke was asked, 'What is a good sermon?' he replied simply, 'A sermon that does good.' Throughout his career as a preacher he spoke spontaneously without preparation, saying that he could never make a sermon before he went into the pulpit. He had a gift for seizing upon any local incident that was known to his audience which he would then use to explain the words of the Bible. What did he try to do in his sermons? His aim was always to make his hearers think deeply about the conduct of their own lives, to ask them to examine their conscience in the light of the word of God. He hoped that he was 'doing good there and then', and so his stories were simple tales used to teach a moral lesson intended to make them better men and women.

Naturally he must have had the typical Methodist gifts for rousing emotions and involving his audience. There would always be the touch of melodrama, the hero, the heroine and the villain, with rescue coming in the nick of time. No one was better at persuading a congregation that they were living in the story than the Methodist preacher George Whitefield. He had hypnotic powers and a fine dramatic sense that could have made him a great actor. On one occasion he compared the unrepentant sinner to a blind old man, moving unawares to the edge of a precipice. The drop was Hellfire. As the edge came nearer the crowd began to shout a warning, but too late. Lord Chesterfield, who was listening, jumped up crying, 'Good God! He's gone!' Another story tells of him preaching to sailors and using the image of a sinking ship: 'the waves crash over her, the masts are going, she is on her beam-ends! What next?' 'The boats! Take to the boats!' cried out the excited audience. This was how the Methodists captured the imagination of eighteenth-century England.

During his time on the Trowbridge Circuit Adam Clarke was known as 'the boy preacher' and was the youngest on the road. He delivered 506 sermons. In the next Methodist Year he was sent to the Norwich Circuit, containing 22 towns and villages in Norfolk and Suffolk involving a round trip of 260 miles. The weather was cold and accommodation uncomfortable. He records that he often slept in the loft of a barn or outhouse, and in one place during a thunderstorm lifted a door off its hinges and sheltered under it for the night. His salary during this year was £12. Norfolk was a county in which the Methodists were unpopular and Clarke always described it as the most ungodly part of the British Empire. Preachers hardly ever got through an evening meeting without having to face the anger of the mob.

In the next year he was sent to the East Cornwall Circuit and rode the 400 miles there with 23 shillings and sixpence as his only resource, most of which went on feeding his horse. Travelling via London he was able to preach at Moorfields, as Wesley had done, but he was relieved to reach St Austell, because in Cornwall Methodism had found one of its strongholds. Crowded congregations received him and thousands came to listen to his sermons; on one evening at St Austell the chapel was so full that he had to get through a back window to reach the pulpit. From Cornwall he went to the Channel Isles, to introduce the faith as a missionary. Again he met with opposition; the Governor threatened to transport him to the Casquets, a rock in the sea nine miles off Alderney, holding nothing but a lighthouse, but Clarke persevered in his work, made about 400 converts and before leaving had built chapels at Alderney and Guernsey. John Wesley had visited him there and preached in both islands.

Adam Clarke never spared himself. Writing to his wife Mary, whom he had married in 1788, he often admitted that he was in poor health and exhausted. An extract from his Journal about that time gives some indication of the strain of such work:

> Yesterday rode from Bath to Bristol, and back again this morning. Met five classes and preached once; have yet to meet six classes and preach twice. Tomorrow morning return to Bristol, as we begin to meet classes at six in the morning, and continue with short intervals the whole of the day, to the end of the week. I feel willing but am almost knocked up. Back to Bristol fatigued and wet; preached at five and met the Society. Next morning at five preached again; and then rode to the Marsh, where, scarcely able to speak, I preached again; from thence to Clutton, through a severe tempest, wet to the skin; scarcely able to move for over an hour after.

Mr Clarke was now well known as a dedicated and stimulating preacher. From this time onwards he was sent to work in large centres of population, bringing hope to people whose working lives were not touched by the regular clergy and who did not attend church. By preaching in the fields he expected to attract those who were curious, and who were drawn by crowds or a show; meetings began with a well known psalm sung by the people, followed by a prayer with his sermon coming at the end, designed to be remembered, and delivered with as much earnestness as he could command. He hoped that many would go away converted.

It is surprising to recall the way in which both the established Church of England and the governing classes disliked the Methodists and their religion of 'enthusiasm'. It is certain that some of the riotous mobs who attacked preachers and attempted to break up their meetings were encouraged by members of the Anglican clergy, who were outraged by their field-preaching and

their enormous congregations. When Adam Clarke preached in Leeds it was said that people had walked 40 miles and all night to be present at his meetings. The population of the town was estimated to have been increased by 20,000 during the summer by preachers and their Classes who had assembled from the neighbouring counties to hear him.

It has often been said that Methodism at this time saved England from revolution. America and France had seen their systems of government overturned. In this country the sudden growth of industrial towns in places which had once been country villages had created problems which eighteenth-century politicians could neither handle nor understand. Many writers of the time speak of the terrible conditions of the poor. The inhabitants of the factory towns lived in a state of bestiality which reduced them to the level of wild animals, in which no mercy was shown to the young, defenceless or crippled. The threat of violence and riot was always present in this wretchedness. Writing about these times 40 years later Clarke himself believed that the movement for factory reform had done as much as Methodism to keep the workers quiet, and that a well run factory contributed to it: 'manufactories are a blessing independently of the means of living which they ensure, as discipline and order which they produce are unnoticed restraints on immorality and vice, and order is Heaven's first law.' He sounds here less like a religious radical than a cautious countryman, but he had just visited Ireland and had seen starvation in the faces of the poor. Industry there, he thought, would give them a better prospect of work and happiness for their families.

John Wesley had died in 1791, two years before this country joined in the European war against France. In these years Clarke found himself in turn appointed to London, Liverpool and Manchester. Two of his

41 John Wesley (1703-1791).

person was a sinner in need of salvation, but good could best be done in a framework of order. Human life was a simple affair — all that a man needed was faith in the saving power of Jesus Christ, and trust in God. As he wrote: 'Mr Wesley had no plan except that of following the openings of Providence. Our doctrine is from the revelation of God and our discipline likewise.'

Wherever he was living with his wife and family he still went as an ordinary member to the local Methodist Class putting down his penny with the newest member. Their numbers were growing: by the turn of the century there were over one hundred thousand Methodists. 'I feel it a great help to forget that I am a preacher and come with a simple heart to receive instruction from my leader.' When he was writing this, Clarke had received every honour which Methodism could bestow. He had not sought it, but he had been President of the Conference and was to be so twice again, he was Superintendent of the London Circuit and he had been honoured by many outside bodies. He was a respected Biblical scholar and translator, an authority on books and manuscripts, Assistant to the British and Foreign Bible Society and a Keeper of the Public Records.

Although his health was failing he continued on the Circuits, from London, to Liverpool, to Dublin and on a mission to the Orkney and Shetland Isles. He was in great demand as a special preacher on occasions such as the opening of new chapels. It was after a visit to Liverpool for such a ceremony that he contracted the cholera from which he died. He knew that he was not strong enough to resist this illness, which was almost incurable at that time, and a few days before his death he wrote: 'I feel a simple heart. The prayers of my childhood are still precious to me, and the simple hymns I sang when a child I sing now with delight. May I be with you to all eternity. Amen. ADAM CLARKE.'

colleagues at this time were the later famous preachers Bradburn and Benson, who took opposing views on the struggle taking place in France, Mr Bradburn seeing it as the fight for liberty against tyranny, while Mr Benson thought of it as anarchy attempting to uproot the foundations of the established order. Clarke agreed with the latter view, as Wesley would have done, for although he once described his political views as those of an independent Whig, this was no more than Pitt himself had been before the revolution broke out.

Mr Clarke did not involve himself in politics: 'We must honour the King and the Constitution', he said, 'the Constitution is good; it is the best under the sun.' He believed in the fundamental equality of mankind in that Methodism taught that every

8 THE SOLDIER:

William Wheeler

Britain spent almost half the eighteenth-century fighting wars on land and sea. Her soldiers and sailors won an empire and defended it. One of these men was Private William Wheeler, of the Fifty First Regiment of Foot, whose letters from the battlefield give us an immediate and first hand account of what life was like for an ordinary infantryman in a typical regiment of that time. Of course, no British soldier ever thinks himself ordinary — whatever jokes he may share about the footsloggers, Fred Karno's Army, the Ragtime Infantry or the P.B.I. — he will be intensely proud of his regiment and his place in it.

Today the Light Infantry, with their headquarters at the Sir John Moore Barracks, Shrewsbury, are the successors of Wheeler's regiment and its traditions. Aged 24, he joined the regular army in 1809, after having been a Volunteer in the Surrey Militia. The regiment had just come back from Spain, where its commander Sir John Moore had been killed in action at Corunna after a daring raid across country to cut the French lines of communication. It was being brought up to strength again with 650 volunteers joining the nucleus of 150 old soldiers who had come back from the Peninsula.

When Wheeler joined, the 51st had been converted into Light Infantry, men who were expected to march and move faster than ordinary regiments. They carried less equipment and were armed with a rifled musket which was more accurate and four pounds lighter in weight than the normal 'Brown Bess' musket. Speed of movement about the battlefield is still an important factor in warfare, but in those days it was vital. The killing range of a musket then was less than a hundred yards, and large armies might manoeuvre within sight of each other for the best fighting position before the battle began. Light infantry could seize and occupy high ground or other vantage points until other troops arrived to take over, and in a retreat they would be the last rearguard to cover the main army.

To join his regiment Wheeler marched with the Volunteer draft from Maidstone to Kingsbridge Barracks, Devon, where he met Colonel Mainwaring, his Commanding Officer, for the first time. Although describing the Colonel as 'humane' as opposed to 'tyrants' he had known — his usual classification for officers — Wheeler's picture of his C.O. reveals a fiercely extrovert and eccentric character whose behaviour was totally unpredictable. Mainwaring was fond of boasting that his men would not only beat the French but eat them afterwards; he was thought a kindly man because he seldom gave more than 75 lashes as a punishment, but he once gave 300 lashes to a man who accidentally spat on him as he was delivering a message. Seeing Wheeler's eyes watering when on parade in the sun he ordered him to double out to the front of the battalion with his shouldered musket and made him drink 3½ oz of Epsom salts brought by the Hospital Sergeant. During one battle he accused his own horse of cowardice and stopped its corn for three days for rearing up when a cannon ball passed under its belly.

He was a brave and proud man, always leading the Charge and despising the fire of the French — like most of Wellington's officers — but he did not escape the censure of his Commander-in-Chief, being relieved of command after the fight at Fuentes D'Onoro for burning the Colours lest they fall into the hands of the enemy. Another of Wheeler's stories is that he ordered the men to fire low, because a man falling wounded and crying for help would get two comrades to carry him away, and this would be three less to fight. Perhaps the French did the same, for Wheeler was shot through both ankles when he was hit at Nivelle in 1813.

In June 1809 Wheeler found himself under orders for foreign service — the Barrack gates had been left open for cowards to desert — but none of his comrades had left him when they paraded for embarkation. His particular mate was Tom Hooker, who had joined with him from the Surreys; they had vowed to stick together when they went into action. At Spithead they boarded

HMS *Impetueuse,* a ship of the line, with one gundeck cleared to accommodate them. He looked round the harbour in amazement and thought there were so many ships and masts that they were like kidney bean sticks in a kitchen garden. The sailors had newly caulked the gundeck and the troops did not go below till dark; 'it was a fine treat for the blue jackets,' says Wheeler, 'to see all the lobsters stuck to the decks' next morning. The expedition was a failure. The Redcoats took Walcheren, an island which protected the river approach to Antwerp, but the navy could not break the iron chains which prevented ships from going up river. Fever was another enemy: 'I am the only man in the company that has escaped the ague,' wrote Wheeler. Packed on a marshy island and unaware of the risks from the malarial mosquito the men had gone sick in hundreds.

Back at Horsham Barracks they took in new recruits and trained up to battle fitness. When they were ready they were reviewed by the Prince of Wales: 'Colonel M. swaggered in front of the Corps like a Bashaw with three tails.' In January 1811 they rejoined Wellington's Peninsular Army in Spain. On their way there, aboard *HMS Revenge,* Wheeler noticed how much better the discipline was on this ship — the sailors called the Captain 'Father' and groups of Methodists among the crew led hymns and prayers. His first letters home from Portugal give the typical reaction of all British soldiers in foreign stations — like Kipling's 'Barrack Room Ballads' or Tommy Atkins writing to the *Wipers Times:*

> What an ignorant, superstitious, priest-ridden, dirty, lousy set of poor Devils are the Portuguese. The filthiest pigsty is a palace to the filthy houses in this dirty, stinking city [of Lisbon].

42 **Assault craft: the regimental band was a vital part of any force which had to march into action.**

61

He marched off to the front in battle order complaining about the weight of kit he had to carry:

> Seven days biscuit, five days meat, two days wine. Every man's kit consisted of one blanket, one watchcoat (a greatcoat), two shirts, two pair of stockings, two pair boots, one pair of soles and heels, besides all the other little etceteras, sixty rounds of ball cartridge in the pouch; all this was load enough for a donkey.

Grumbling at everything he went into action at Fuentes D'Onoro, one of Wellington's less well-controlled battles, in which the 51st was caught on a reverse slope by French cavalry. Colonel Mainwaring had behaved with great coolness and gallantry, but Wellington sent him home; Major Rice, who had lost his right hand in an earlier fight, took command. Wheeler used to write his letters for him. At Fuentes Wheeler

43 'Ensign Dyas and the Stormers' at San Cristoval, Badajoz. This toast is still drunk in the Mess of the King's Own Yorkshire Light Infantry.

himself came through unscathed and cheerful — in real danger he always thought life well worth living — just as he did in the attack on the Fort of San Cristoval at Badajoz. This episode is still remembered today in the Regiment, when on dinner nights they drink a toast to 'Ensign Dyas and the Stormers'.

Dyas was a young, penniless Irish officer in the 51st who had nothing to lose but his life, and everything to gain by volunteering to lead a storming party to climb the walls and capture the place. He tried three times but failed. Wheeler was in the second raid. As men fell around him and their scaling ladders would not reach the top of the walls Wheeler found himself cut off by French troops making a sortie. It was dark, so he fell flat and rubbed his haversack into the bodies around him until it was soaked in blood.

62

He put the pack on his back and shammed dead, lying with his face in the mud, while unseen enemy hands pulled off his boots, stockings and shirt. Whenever our guns fired and the French took cover he got up and ran. By daybreak he was back in his own lines in time to stop his name from being posted in the 'dead and missing' list. Dyas was promoted to Lieutenant for his bravery in this action.

Like every good soldier Wheeler had the knack of making a hard and bloody life as comfortable as possible. Before he marched from Brussels to fight at Waterloo he was enjoying 'plenty of good grub, gin and tobacco and all for nix'. He had a fatalistic approach to death: 'The best way is to enjoy ourselves while we can, it will be time to bid the Devil good morning when we meet him.' Of course he was lucky — at Nivelles in 1813 he received a wound which temporarily disabled him but which was hardly serious until it turned septic in hospital. He was shot through the right ankle by a bullet which had already taken flesh off his left. As he fell his comrade on the left, Ned Eagan, was shot dead and fell on top of him. Tom Hooker on his right stood by to defend them both but had to move back with his company. Again Wheeler had his pockets picked by a French soldier, but as the latter went on working over the casualties for loot Wheeler picked up Eagan's loaded gun and killed him. Minutes later the battle turned and the British came storming back, so he crawled over to the Frenchman and recovered his money and more besides.

We do not know how Wheeler was able to write like this. That he was a relatively well educated man for his time and station in life is clear. He seems to have been a farm worker before enlisting. His officers always knew that he could read and write well. When he was in hospital at St Jean de Luz the Commandant had him working as his personal clerk, the doctor used him to check the medical records and the Commis-sariat branch made him Acting Quartermaster Sergeant. Like many soldiers before and since, Bill Wheeler did not want promotion. He enjoyed life without responsibility; the NCOs might give the orders but when things went wrong they usually got the blame. Officers told him he was a fool for refusing stripes, but to offers of rank and women his reply was the same: 'Your humble servant does not intend to get entangled with any of them.'

Whenever the campaigning was over and the army was in billets Wheeler was alive to the delights of the landscape and the pleasures of the fireside. He thought the vineyards and the olive trees wonderful and was fascinated by the variety of the wild life, especially by the colours of the lizards. From his notes it would seem that the regiment kept pairs of greyhounds to put up game for the pot, and that this was sometimes done when troops were on the march. With the Portuguese and Spaniards he was the prince of confidence tricksters,

44 A camp-follower with her children: this was not Wheeler's way — 'when a soldier's hat is on his family is covered'.

selling army blankets literally off the men's backs to the townsfolk. This was undetected; the trick was to cut a blanket in half and pad out the remaining half with fern when on parade. In action blankets could easily be taken from the fallen.

In trading with the Portuguese Wheeler always pretended he was Irish, thereby getting a better deal, and occasionally in billets he had been known to sprinkle gunpowder along the hearth to produce an explosion which frightened away the occupants and gave the troops full enjoyment of the fireside. He would not have tried any tricks like this on the women in camp, who were expert foragers and fighters among themselves and were sometimes widowed three times over in a campaign. When the battle in which he was hit was over he got into a nearby house for a sleep and chalked 'Provost Martial' on the door, which discouraged any wandering marauders from disturbing him. He knew how to play the old soldier!

Like other men in other wars he had a great respect for the enemy Commander-in-Chief, whom he called Napoleon the Great, whereas he despised 'Old Bungy Louis' whom the Allies restored to the throne of France after Waterloo. Wheeler could be as savage as a tiger when need be but did not go looking for a fight, and tells one tale about the two armies being encamped with an inviting apple orchard between them — men from both sides went in to pick apples and were eventually picking from the same trees. In hospital at Fuenterrabia he struck up a friendship with a French Corporal Pipin, who was an educated man, spoke perfect English and was an excellent cook. Their friendship survived the strain of Wheeler's discovering that the tasty fat rabbit which he had just enjoyed, cooked in the French fashion, had in fact been the hospital cat.

Invalided back to England he was still unfit when the French war ended and the Peninsular veterans were shipped to America. Wellington always said that this was Britain's finest army, and for men like Wheeler 'Old Nosey' was the only man to match Napoleon — his strategy in Spain had been beyond the men in the ranks — Wheeler thought it amazing that after marching for days they would suddenly be deployed into battle formations in a good position and find the French appearing out of an empty landscape.

He knew that he was lucky to be alive for he had agreed to his leg being amputated after becoming infected, but a Spanish doctor insisted on his own dressing, which proved antiseptic and saved his leg. A sergeant's wife who was nursing in the ward pricked her finger with a needle left in the bandages; the finger became septic and was amputated, but the infection had travelled to her hand, which was amputated, only to find her arm poisoned. She refused more surgery and died soon afterwards.

Before leaving Spain Wheeler went to see a bullfight at Irun, which he described as a different way of bull-baiting, but he eventually got back to Portsmouth in September 1814: 'the evening was spent with song and glass, and after drowning our cares in good old English October we retired to rest.'

By March 1815 he was back on active service, which he always preferred: 'The sooner the campaign opens the better. It is true we shall have to encounter great dangers and fatigue. What of that, it is the very life of a soldier to keep moving. If we do suffer privations at times we have some sunshiney days.' Napoleon had escaped from Elba and was back in France. Wheeler had been promoted to Sergeant. He could not object this time — he was a veteran and experienced men were needed. The regiment

45 Plan of Waterloo: the Allies were deployed facing south along the forward slope of the hill, witn fortified villages and farms in front; the French had to attack uphill, across soft ground.

64

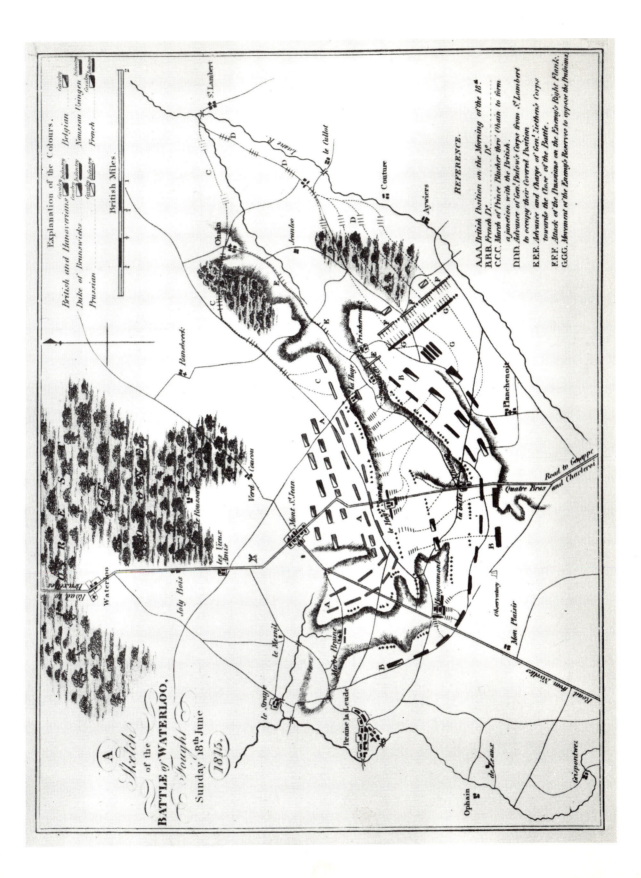

A Sketch of the BATTLE of WATERLOO, Fought Sunday 18th June 1815.

Explanation of the Colours.

British and Hanoverians — British Infantry — British Cavalry
Duke of Brunswicks
Prussian

Belgian
Nassau Usingen
French

British Miles.

REFERENCE.

AAA British Position on the Morning of the 18th.
BBB French Do. Do.
CCC March of Prince Blucher thro' Ohain to form a junction with the British.
DDD Advance of Gen.l Bulow's Corps from S.t Lambert to occupy their covered Position.
EEE Advance and Charge of Gen.l Zietten's Corps towards the Close of the Battle.
FFF Attack of the Prussians on the Enemy's Right Flank.
GGG Movement of the Enemy's Reserve to oppose the Prussians.

was still commanded by Colonel Rice and was part of Colville's Fourth Division; Wheeler's Brigade would fight on the right, with Hanoverians in the centre and another British Brigade on the left. They had landed at Ostend and been ferried by canal barge to Ghent, from where they had marched to Brussels. Napoleon was on the move and the Prince of Orange was in command of the British Army.

This did not suit Wheeler, nor others like him. He had met up with a few old hands who had been in Spain. Again they agreed to stick together in action and share out any booty they picked up. In the Peninsula Wheeler's best single haul had been 652 Spanish dollars, but he had to split it 16 ways — all he had picked up so far on the march was a purse of coins dropped by a Belgian cavalryman galloping through Nivelles. But their spirits were high because Wellington was back: 'Glorious news, Nosey has got the command, won't we give them a drubbing now, drink hearty to the health of our old commander, we don't care a damn for all France.'

When he wrote home again after the 'three day fight' he did not know that this would be called the Waterloo campaign. The regiment had been fortunate in losing only nine killed and about 40 wounded, whereas for the army as a whole one man in every six had been a casualty. The 51st had been on high ground on the right flank of the line of battle. The farm of Hougoumont, held by the Guards, was to their left and in front of them. During the night before the battle they had been so close to the enemy, said Wheeler, that they could not light fires or sleep: 'We sat on our knapsacks until daylight, there was no shelter against the weather: the water ran in streams from the cuffs of our jackets.' Had he known it the wet weather had greatly helped the allied cause, for the ground had softened so much by morning that Napoleon waited for it to dry out before attacking. Thick mud would

stop his artillery from manoeuvring quickly and his cavalry from charging, but during the time he wasted the Prussians were marching to Wellington's aid.

So far as Wheeler was concerned he took post among cornfields with a sunken road running across his front. When the artillery bombardment started his men were moved forward into the sunken road and were hidden by the high rye grass. The battle raged to their left and their main danger came from French cavalry coming down the road after Ney's famous charge midway through the afternoon had broken on the British Squares. About 100 French Cuirassiers came down the road towards the 51st, and every man and horse was shot down. Earlier in the day a single French Hussar scout had approached Wheeler's company within range of the dead shot Private Chipping. They got 40 double Napoleons from his body and tore the gold braid off his uniform.

By dusk Prussian cavalry was passing them and they followed up to Hougoumont, where British Guards lay dead in heaps, and where they realized that the French were beaten and retreating. On the following day they were joined by the rest of the Fourth Division which had been in reserve at Hal. They went on to occupy Cambrai and began the long march to Paris, where they were billeted by the Seine in the Bois de Boulogne and had a merry time: 'I anticipate enjoying the happiest summer I ever had in my life,' wrote Wheeler. He deserved it, for men like him had won the greatest war Britain had fought up to that time, and had made their country supreme in Europe.

47 Napoleon, defeated in his first and only battle against Wellington, escapes from the battlefield.

List of dates

1714 George Lewis, Elector of Hanover, succeeds as King George I.
1715 Jacobite rising of 'The Old Pretender'; Crosby Hall searched.
1716 Nicholas Blundell leaves for Flanders. Richard Kay born at Bury.
1719 The Blundells return. Lord and Lady Westmorland visit Crosby.
1721 Walpole becomes Prime Minister.
1723 The Blundells bring their daughters home from Flanders.
1727 George II succeeds. Queen Caroline of Anspach loyal to Walpole.
1728 Last entry in Blundell's *Great Diurnal*, begins new Tenants' Book.
1733 Walpole's Excise Bill defeated. John Kay of Bury patents the Flying Shuttle.
1737 Deaths of Queen Caroline and Nicholas Blundell. Richard Kay joins his father's practice.
1740 War with France; Frederick II attacks Silesia; Arne's *Rule Britannia*.
1743 George II defeats the French at Dettingen. Richard Kay goes to Guy's Hospital.
1744 Anson's voyage round the world. Kay hears Wesley preach, qualifies as surgeon.
1745 Jacobite rebellion; Kay sees Highlanders in Manchester; *God Save The King*.
1748 Peace of Aix-la-Chapelle. Kay's riding accident in Rossendale.

1749 Handel's *Music for the Royal Fireworks*. Harry Carter born at Pengersick.
1750 Betty Berkeley born at Charborough, Dorset. Richard Kay's father dies.
1751 Clive at Arcot. Deaths of Prince of Wales, Richard Kay and his mother and sister.
1755 Johnson's Dictionary published. 51st Foot formed at Leeds as Brudenell's Regiment.
1756 Seven Years War begins. Peter Stubs born in Warrington.
1760 George III, grandson of George II, succeeds. Adam Clarke born at Moybeg, Derry.
1765 Stamp Act. Harry Carter first goes smuggling.
1767 Betty Berkeley marries William, later sixth Baron Craven.
1773 Boston Tea Party. Carter commands his first ship.
1776 American Declaration of Independence. Ellen Weeton born at Lancaster.
1777 Stubs marries Mary Sutton.
1778 War with France; Carter imprisoned at St Malo. Clarke joins the Methodists.
1779 War with Spain. Carter brothers released from prison.
1780 Gordon Riots. Betty Berkeley leaves her husband; her play produced at Drury Lane.

1782 Lord North resigns. Rodney's victories; Tom Weeton killed in action.

1783 Peace of Versailles. Betty Berkeley's Grand Tour. Adam Clarke on Trowbridge Circuit.

1784 Pitt the Younger becomes Prime Minister. Mary Weeton moves to Up Holland.

1785 Watt's Steam Engine with rotary motion. William Wheeler born.

1786 Betty Berkeley goes to Anspach. Carter marries Elizabeth Flindel. Clarke in Channel Isles.

1787 Carter fights *Black Prince* privateer. Stubs takes the *White Bear* Inn.

1788 *The Times* founded. Mary Weeton's school opens. Clarke marries Mary Cook.

1789 French Revolution begins. Carter in Baltimore. Clarke on Leeds Circuit.

1790 Margrave of Anspach and Betty Berkeley visit Prussian court.

1791 John Wesley dies. Betty Berkeley marries at Lisbon.

1792 Carter operating three cutters from Guernsey, owns a house at Roscoff.

1793 War with France; Carter imprisoned. Betty Berkeley becomes Princess of the Holy Roman Empire.

1795 Carter released and returned to England. Clarke preaching in Manchester.

1797 Naval mutinies. Death of Mary Weeton. Margrave of Anspach buys Benham Valence.

1799 Stubs part-owner of vessels trading with the Baltic.

1802 Peace of Amiens. Betty Berkeley in Paris. Stubs sets up new workshops in Warrington.

1806 Deaths of Pitt, the Margrave of Anspach and Peter Stubs.

1807 Clarke becomes Chairman of the London Circuit.

1808 Ellen Weeton closes school at Up Holland.

1809 Wheeler joins 51st Foot; Walcheren expedition.

1810 Ellen Weeton at Ambleside.

1811 Prince of Wales becomes Regent. 51st Light Infantry engaged at Fuentes D'Onoro and San Cristoval.

1812 Badajoz stormed; Battle of Salamanca. Ellen Weeton climbs Snaefell.

1813 Battle of Vitoria; San Sebastian taken; Corporal Wheeler wounded at Nivelles.

1814 Sergeant Wheeler re-joins the 51st before Waterloo. Mary Stock born.

1820 Prince Regent succeeds as George IV.

1822 Ellen Weeton leaves Aaron Stock and returns to Up Holland.

1825 Ellen Weeton climbs Snowdon. Betty Berkeley re-visits Benham Valence.

1828 Death of Betty Berkeley in Naples. Wheeler invalided out of King's Own Light Infantry at Corfu.

1829 Harry Carter dies at Rinsey.

1830 Death of George IV, succeeded by his brother William IV.

Book list

The following were used to find the inform-
ation for this book:

Ashton, T.S., *An Early Industrialist: Peter
    Stubs of Warrington,* Manchester, 1939
Bagley, J.J., *Lancashire Diarists: Three
    Centuries of Lancashire Lives,* Phillimore,
    1975
Broadley, A.M., and Melville, L., *The Beauti-
    ful Lady Craven,* Bodley Head, 1913
Brockbank, W., and Kenworthy, F., *The
    Diary of Richard Kay of Baldingstone,*
    The Chetham Society, 1968
Cornish, J.B., *The Autobiography of a
    Cornish Smuggler: Captain Harry Carter
    of Prussia Cove,* Bradford Barton Ltd.,
    Truro, 1894, reprinted 1971
Etheridge, J.W., *Life of Adam Clarke,*
    London, 1859
Fulford, R., *Royal Dukes,* Pan Books, 1948
Hall, E., (ed.), *Miss Weeton: Journal of a
    Governess,* Oxford University Press, 1936
Liddell Hart, B.H., *The Letters of Private
    Wheeler, 1809-1828,* Joseph, 1951
Owen, J.B., *The Eighteenth Century 1714-
    1815,* Nelson, 1974
Plumb, J.H., *The First Four Georges,* Bats-
    ford, 1956
Turberville, A.S., *Englishmen and Manners
    in the Eighteenth Century,* Galaxy, 1957
Tyrer, F., *The Great Diurnal of Nicholas
    Blundell,* The Record Society of Lanca-
    shire and Cheshire, 1968

Some other books on the Georgian Period:

Sources and illustrations

Briggs, A., *How They Lived, 1700-1815,*
    Blackwell, 1969
Edwards, T.C., and Richardson, B., (ed.),
    They Saw It Happen 1689-1897, Black-
    well, 1958
Millward, J.S., *Portraits and Documents:
    The Eighteenth Century,* Hutchinson,
    1962
Royston Pike, E., *Human Documents of the
    Industrial Revolution in Britain,* Allen
    and Unwin, 1966
Woodforde, J., *The Diary of a Country
    Parson, 1758-1802,* Oxford University
    Press, 1949
Williams Ellis, A., and Stobbs, W., *Life in
    England,* Blackie, 1970

Textbooks: political, social and economic

Cootes, R.J., *Britain Since 1700,* Longman
Holland, A.J., *The Age of Industrial Expan-
    sion,* Nelson
Moss, P., *History Alive,* Blond
Neal, T.A., *From the Restoration to
    Regency, 1660-1815,* Nelson
Parreaux, A., *Daily Life in England in the
    Reign of George III,* Allen and Unwin
Quennell, M., and C.B., *A History of Every-
    day Things in England,* Batsford

There are relevant volumes on the eighteenth century in the following series:

The Clarendon Biographies, Oxford University Press
Then and There, Longman
People of the Past (fiction based on fact) Oxford University Press

Academic works

Ashton, T.S., *The Industrial Revolution, 1760-1830,* Oxford University Press, 1948
Marshall, D., *Eighteenth-Century England,* Longman, 1962
Plumb, J.H., *England in the Eighteenth Century,* Penguin, 1950
Watson, J.S., *The Reign of George III,* Oxford University Press, 1960

Index

The numbers in **bold** type refer to the figure numbers of the illustrations